MW01051440

Career Moves might just be the most important business/life book that has come along in our day and age…it's genius! Read this book if you want to maximize the opportunity that is waiting at your door.

—BOB BURG
COAUTHOR OF *THE GO-GIVER* AND *GO-GIVERS SELL MORE*

Proactive, affirming, filled with love…this is how Dondi Scumaci lives her life. Her exceptional gift is sharing the secrets of her success with all of us!

—ELIZABETH HENNICK
PRESIDENT, TRAINING EVOLUTION, INC.

Career Moves is another example of Dondi's commitment to making a positive difference in the lives of women in the workplace. All companies need people who can survey the terrain ahead, create opportunities, and navigate challenges. Dondi's new book incorporates an illustrative story line filled with practical advice to help her audience become these critical individuals. *Career Moves* provides valuable insights helping those with dedication, intelligence, and desire to reach their full career potential.

—BETH A. BAILEY
EXECUTIVE VICE PRESIDENT AND
CHIEF ADMINISTRATION OFFICER, CB&I

CAREER
MOVES

CAREER
MOVES

DONDI SCUMACI

EXcel
BOOKS
A STRANG COMPANY

Most STRANG COMMUNICATIONS BOOK GROUP products are available at special quantity discounts for bulk purchase for sales promotions, premiums, fund-raising, and educational needs. For details, write Strang Communications Book Group, 600 Rinehart Road, Lake Mary, Florida 32746, or telephone (407) 333-0600.

CAREER MOVES by Dondi Scumaci
Published by Excel Books
A Strang Company
600 Rinehart Road
Lake Mary, Florida 32746
www.strangbookgroup.com

Unless otherwise noted, all Scripture quotations are from the New American Standard Bible. Copyright © 1960, 1962, 1963, 1968, 1971, 1972, 1973, 1975, 1977, 1995 by the Lockman Foundation. Used by permission. (www.Lockman.org)

People and incidents in this book are composites created by the author for her experiences in speaking and consulting. Names and details of the stories have been changed, and any similarity between the names and stories of individuals described in this book to individuals known to readers is purely coincidental.

Cover design by Amanda Potter
Design Director: Bill Johnson

Library of Congress Cataloging-in-Publication Data

Scumaci, Dondi.
  Career moves / Dondi Scumaci.
      p. cm.
  Includes bibliographical references.
  ISBN 978-1-59979-857-8
  1. Christian women--Religious life. 2. Women employees--
Religious life. 3. Unemployed women workers--Religious life. 4. Job
satisfaction--Religious aspects--Christianity. I. Title.
  BV4527.S288 2010
  248.8'43--dc22

                                        2009048554

First Edition

10 11 12 13 14 — 9 8 7 6 5 4 3 2 1
Printed in the United States of America

This book is dedicated to women who recognize the signs and have the courage to make the moves. It is also for mentors everywhere—men and women who invest themselves so beautifully in the lives and careers of others. You are making such a marvelous difference!

For Courtney and Katelynne, two bright lights in my life—may all of your moves be blessed of God!

ACKNOWLEDGMENTS

I AM KEEN ON acknowledgments because this book (and the two before it) would not have happened without extraordinary people standing next to me.

My family is the best support team on the planet. You are all precious beyond words—even for someone who spends so much time looking for the right words to write and say. Thank you to my husband, Scumaci; my son, Tabor; our lovely Crissy; mothers Elle and Johnny; my father, Rick; and brother, Dean.

Denise Raley, your perspective impacted this work beautifully. You have changed my story in significant ways, and I am grateful.

Thank you to my publisher, Strang Book Group. Behind that name is a group of people who have encouraged, prayed, pulled, and pushed. I am grateful for the invitation and the opportunity to write under your business banner, Excel Books. From *Designed for Success* to *Ready, Set...Grow!* and now *Career Moves*, it has been an honor to partner with you.

I still remember the day I received your message, Barbara Dycus. I was sitting on the bench at an airport, waiting for my car, weary to the bone. With nothing else to do, I checked my voice mail one last time for the day; there you were—talking about the books and your vision for them. It was frightening and thrilling all at the same time. Thousands of words (more than 174,000) have passed between us now, but I will always remember the first words and how they made me feel. Challenged. Energized. Refreshed. Thank you for finding me and opening that door. I am grateful.

In almost every state and on four continents I have worked with and have been surrounded by the most fantastic organizations and the most incredible people. Thank you for sharing your stories, asking your questions, and helping me write a book about how to be successful—wherever you are, right where you are.

Finally, I want to acknowledge you, the reader. This book is for you, and I pray that it will give you exactly what you need in this moment to press on, press through, stand out, and create something extraordinary with your work. I do believe in reinvention! I also believe it is never too late to begin. Shall we?

CONTENTS

Contents

Contents

FOREWORD

YOU MIGHT BE wondering why the foreword to a book that is obviously speaking to women is being written by a man. Actually, I'm sort of wondering that myself. I only know that Dondi Scumaci has honored me by asking me to do this. And if Dondi asks me to do anything, the answer is absolutely and immediately, "Yes."

At the time of this foreword I've actually yet to meet her in person. I know her only through a friendship on Twitter (a popular social and business media site) and via e-mails. But, it doesn't matter. My respect and admiration for her, her work, and her mission are as though I've been a part of her life and family forever and as though she has been a part of mine.

It was obvious from the moment I "met" her and began communicating with her and our mutual Twitter friends why she is so loved and respected by everyone who knows her. She is a giver—a "go-giver," if you will. She doesn't give in order to get; she gives in order to give even more—to build, to edify, to help, and to serve her family, her friends, her readers, and her students—many of whom are at least three of the preceding.

She is an extremely successful former member of the corporate world who accomplished what she teaches in the book. She now focuses on helping other women achieve similar success, whether a part of corporate life or a small, independent business. What a blessing! And, just as she'll show you how to do, she continues to receive in abundance as a direct result of the immense value she provides to countless others.

While I love all her teachings, her latest work—the book you are holding in your hands—might just be the most important business/life book that has come along in our day and age. Dondi has brilliantly wrapped an exciting story of one woman's journey to break through her own self-imposed barriers and achieve greatness inside of a how-to book. It's genius—both in form and in how you'll easily see that if "Zoe" can do it, you can too!

And, again, while I realize it was written with today's career-advancing woman in mind, there is not a person of either gender I know who couldn't benefit from the wisdom contained in *Career Moves*.

You see, like any universal law that contains principles of success, the information must, by the very "definition of the thing," work for everyone who applies it and in any area in which it is applied. You could take any aspect of your life, be it financial, physical, spiritual, mental, emotional, social, relational, and, yes, career, and by simply applying the fundamentals as well as the specifics our amazing teacher and mentor, Ms. Scumaci, so generously shares, become a hugely successful human being.

If you're a woman reading *Career Moves*, the fact that it was written with you in mind is simply a gift. If you're a man reading this book, I encourage you to "cheat" (and I absolutely mean that tongue-in-cheek) and devour the information yourself. And then go out and buy a copy for every woman whose life you'd like to have a hand in helping reach its fullest potential.

Indeed, you are on the threshold—the threshold of success in whatever form you desire! Read this book if you want to maximize the opportunity that is waiting at your door.

—BOB BURG
COAUTHOR OF *THE GO-GIVER* AND *GO-GIVERS SELL MORE*

PROLOGUE

The automatic doors rolled open as they had a hundred times over the past six months with her "comings" and "goings." This was very different—it wasn't just another going; it was an ending. This was her final exit.

A cold January wind slapped her in the face just as the doors closed unceremoniously behind her. "Isn't that just the perfect metaphor?" she thought bitterly. "A cold slap in the face as a door slams behind you."

She made her way across the employee parking lot, picking carefully over treacherous-looking patches of ice. Now the sarcastic voice in her head was gathering real steam: "Another fitting metaphor: Watch your step, or you'll find yourself sprawled all over the pavement of life. Perfect. This is just so absolutely perfect."

Her feet nearly came out from under her just then, and she flailed around ridiculously. She couldn't bear to imagine who might have seen that charming display of grace.

Now she sat motionless in her car, letting the engine warm, the windows defrost, and reality climb slowly over her. "Let go," she stiffly recited to an icy windshield. "After further review, I've been released from my position." Another image popped into her head like a thought bubble in a comic strip. "I've been released from the prison of my dead-end job."

How did she not see this coming? She felt the indignation rising. How could they do this to her? It was so unfair!

She really shouldn't be surprised. The past few months had been pretty miserable. What started as a "great job" had become a thankless chore. On most days it took every drop of personal discipline to drag her body through that door and chain herself to that desk. The prison image popped up again; she tried very hard to ignore it. That picture was not at all helpful.

Her mind flipped through the pages of her "on-the-job" experience. She remembered how nervous she had been the day she had interviewed for the position and how thrilled she had been to get the job. She would have accepted any position to get her foot in the door of that company. (Come to think of it, she had.) Some opportunity it had turned out to be! The work wasn't hard; it was boring and repetitive and mindless.

She had taken an entry-level position, confident that she would quickly prove herself and earn a promotion. It hadn't taken long at all to discover someone would have to quit, die, or retire in order for her to advance one inch! As the pages turned in her mind, she saw the slow march from completely thrilled...to dreading Mondays.

A gear shifted in her brain as she reasoned with the windshield. "This is so unfair! I did everything asked of me. They were lucky to have me. Losing this stupid job is probably the best thing that has ever happened to me."

The windshield offered no assurance, and the feeling sitting in her throat certainly wasn't relief. It was fear, embarrassment, and hurt twisted into one big knot of ugly emotion. As she pulled out of the parking lot for the last time, the full force of it slammed into her.

What she didn't understand was the amazing journey before her, whom she would encounter on the path, what she would learn along the way…and how utterly unprepared she was for this trip.

one

MOVING SIGNS

Get Ready to Make Your Move!

From her office on the seventh floor, Alena watched Zoe go.

Once the young woman nearly slipped on the ice, and Alena held her breath just a bit. She thought about the days leading up to this moment and sighed as she thought about those virtual "slips and slides." It had been very hard to watch Zoe fall.

More than once Alena had reached out, trying to help Zoe find her balance at work. If Zoe noticed the attempts, she had given no indication. She actually seemed oblivious to her peril. "At least she sees the ice underfoot now," Alena mused. "She's choosing her steps more carefully now."

Zoe was very bright; there was no argument there. She had great energy and potential. Alena was honestly sorry to see her go. Still, it was the right decision; she was certain of that. Zoe had not taken hold of the opportunity presented to her, and now it had literally slipped away. While she had not managed Zoe directly,

5

she had seen her work and often hoped to see more effort and ownership.

This organization placed high premiums on innovation, resourcefulness, personal leadership, and initiative. Employees were expected to connect with the strategies and find ways to "plug themselves in" at every level. Zoe had not demonstrated these attributes. She had approached her job from a "just-tell-me-what-you-want-me-to-do-and-I-will-do-it" perspective.

Because she had not looked for ways to engage, Zoe's role was reduced to the most routine tasks. She seemed satisfied to set up the conference room and prepare handouts for staff and client meetings. "I wish you had shown an interest in the purpose of those meetings," thought Alena. "You seemed to know what to do, but you missed the 'why' entirely."

Zoe finally reached her car and was letting the engine warm.

"We are not looking for order takers here, Zoe. We are looking for leaders—at every level," Alena said aloud as Zoe's car finally pulled away.

Worse than losing Zoe was Alena's suspicion that the lessons had not been learned. If that were true, they would be repeated again and again.

"Perhaps not," she said to herself. "Maybe we can still alter the course." She returned to her desk and wrote a brief note before gathering her things and calling it a day.

Do You Recognize the Moving Signs?

Moving signs signal change. Typically, a moving sign in your life means it's time to pack your boxes, sell your junk, and say your good-byes. As they relate to your career, moving signs might work a bit differently. They do signal change—but they don't always require boxes, sales, and farewells.

It's quite possible to "move" inside the job you have, because the move may not require a change in company or position. It might require a change in mind-set, approach, skill sets, attitude, or perceptions. You may even find it necessary to reinvent the job you have in order to get the job you want! (Even as I write this book I am personally responding to my own moving signs! My title won't be changing, and I will still be working from the same locations, but *what* I do and *how* I do it must change. That's uncomfortable and humbling and . . . so worth it!)

In my book *Designed for Success*, I introduced the "Ten Commandments for Women in the Workplace" using an analogy: "Wouldn't it be wonderful if our careers came with a personal navigation system? I love the idea of a friendly voice saying, 'Prepare to turn ahead.' If I missed an opportunity or made a 'career-limiting' move, the still friendly voice would say, 'Recalculating route.' Imagine hearing the words, 'You have arrived!'"[1] Unfortunately, our careers don't have navigation systems on board. If we are paying attention, we may notice the signs, but it's quite possible to miss them entirely or simply ignore them. I think that's tragic! If you miss the sign, you'll miss the turn and the opportunity!

In the spirit of paying attention, I've been collecting moving signs. In conferences around the world and in private consultations, I've asked thousands of people, "What are the signals that tell you it's time to make a career move?"

The answers I hear are as unique as the people who share them. Signs are personal things. They come in all shapes and sizes, but I've found nine common themes. Do any of these resonate with you?

1. You feel a generalized discontent.

What begins on the edge of awareness slowly slides to front and center. This reminds me of a child tugging on your shirttail, quietly (at first) vying for your attention. If you don't listen, "Discontent" will raise "her" voice until you do.

At first, this sign is easy to ignore, because you may be in a very comfortable place. Things are generally OK—except for that bothersome little voice telling you something needs to change; there's more for you to do. Tasks may be getting done, but the work isn't rewarding. It doesn't bring a sense of achievement or accomplishment. It doesn't bring you joy. The work has become an obligation rather than a passion. Instead of energizing you, it exhausts you!

2. You can't get there from here.

This one is easy to spot. If you have a clear plan for your career, and your work isn't building a bridge to that future place, it's time to reevaluate. "Can't-get-there-from-here" problems are frustrating because they may require a dramatic shift to correct the course. You may have to move over, down, or out to get yourself back on track.

We find ourselves in "bridgeless" situations when we accept jobs "out of our context." That means we jump to accept a position without considering how it relates to our path over the long term. We may make that leap out of pure necessity or end up here because we didn't have a plan or a vision to begin with. When organizations downsize, merge, or reorganize, employees may be pushed off their career path to accommodate the change. And sometimes jobs just don't turn into what we thought they would become. (What looked like a bridge from a distance turned out to be a wall.)

People sometimes ignore this sign because it's discouraging to think about starting over or moving "backward." Proceed with caution! Ignoring this signal will lead to some of the signs to follow.

3. You've quit on the job.

Many people quit their jobs without tendering a resignation. I'm not talking about leaving without giving proper notice; I'm talking about disengagement. This is when you keep showing up, but you don't bring yourself to the work. (This sign has integrity and credibility notices attached to it, because you are still collecting a paycheck and your employer isn't aware you've vacated your position.)

If you've quit on the job, it's possible you passed another of the signs sometime back without making a course correction. Down the road, many of the signs look a lot like giving up, giving in, and selling out.

4. There's too much pressure or not enough pressure.

Jobs have "seasons." In our work lives, we go through periods of stretching, balancing, and maintaining. After a time of extreme growth and challenge, we need relief from the pressure. This allows us to stabilize and refresh.

This reminds me of flying a kite. Tension on the line allows the kite to fly. If the tension is too great, the string will snap. If there is no tension on the line, the kite can't take off. *Too much or not enough tension will have the same result—a grounded kite.* The same is true with our jobs. If the pressure is constant with no opportunity to rest, or if there is no pressure to reach, we cannot take off.

Pressure is the gauge. You may need to dial it up or dial it down. Dialing it up may mean seeking challenge; dialing it down may require negotiating some things off your plate, asking for help, or establishing more realistic boundaries.

5. You are off the radar.

This sign may be difficult to find because you are doing just fine. The problem isn't your work; it's what you are working on. Your projects and assignments run off the radar, and that can make you feel "invisible." If you recognize this sign, it may be time to raise your hand and ask for a new challenge, get involved in a critical project, or find new ways to bring greater value to your business partners.

If you are in a support position, for example, providing the information for people on the front line, you might look for ways to make the information more user-friendly and valuable. If you are serving others behind the scenes, find a way to serve them better. Become a partner in success. I often hear this, "I support the team, but I don't feel like I am *on* the team." Put yourself on the radar by getting on the team.

6. Your job doesn't fit your life.

I am inspired by stories of people who looked this sign squarely in the eye and made (sometimes dramatic) changes by tailoring their work to fit their lives. This is a values-based sign. Some make this move to find a better balance between home and work. Others are motivated by their passions.

A dynamic life coach puts it this way: "My career move happened because of my appetite for challenge and innovation. It wasn't reasonable for me to expect the organization I worked for to feed that hunger. The change was up to me."

7. Your job doesn't fit you.

This one hurts because it means your skills aren't suited for the position you're in. What you can do well isn't in your job description. Like a fish out of water struggling to breathe, you are banked.

The most devastating thing about this sign is what happens to your confidence in the process. The longer you stay in a bad fit, the more inadequate you feel. Your confidence takes a real beating. Repeat after me, "A bad job fit does not make me inadequate or less valuable!" This sign should really say, "Get back in the water. You know how to swim."

8. You're settling.

This sign resembles some of the others, but it is different all the same. You have settled when your strengths and gifts are not being used on the job but your comfort zone holds you there. A Gallop Poll found that 87 percent of people employed by corporations believe they are not getting to use their number one talent in their jobs![2]

Hey, we all like to be comfortable—present company included. I'm not even suggesting that you leave your zone of comfort entirely; I do encourage you to expand it! Push the edges out and make room for more!

9. Your motives have malice.

Only "grown-ups" can face this sign. It is not for those who are weak in the knees, happily playing the victim role, or engaged in a game of blame. This one requires confronting yourself at the core of your intentions.

When relationships or situations have become adversarial and you no longer want the people around you to win—when you need others to be wrong so you can be right—it really is time to bust a move.

This is not an all-inclusive list—perhaps you have a sign of your own to add. That's one of the ways to make this book a personal journey. Use what is here to discover your own signals and solutions.

Ultimately, *Career Moves* is about recognizing and responding to your signs! These are the tools that will allow you to get in the driver's seat, take charge of your career, and achieve your goals. As Zoe's story unfolds, so shall yours. Your story will be uniquely your own. Here you are an author, an editor, and a publisher. You will tell your story through the discoveries you make, the actions you take, the decisions you own, and the impact you have.

In *Designed for Success* and *Ready, Set... Grow!* I emphasized the personal process through journaling and self-discovery. You will find those elements in *Career Moves* as well. Each chapter includes a "Get Your Move On!" feature. This is designed to assist you in personal application, and I hope you will accept the assignments!

You'll also notice a new layer of exploration—community.

As you read, I encourage you to think about how you can connect with and contribute to the community of women who are searching for and experiencing breakthrough. You have something to offer this growing community, and it has something to offer in return.

Somewhere down the road, I hope you will look back and see how far you've come and the difference you've made. Chances are you will see something else too—the path you've created for yourself has given others the inspiration to set out on journeys of their own.

Let's pick up the journey with a look at how the workforce is changing, what employers are looking for, and what that means to you and, most importantly, *for you.*

RESPOND TO THE SIGNALS OF CHANGE TO MAKE YOURSELF MORE EMPLOYABLE (AND VALUABLE) IN THE LONG TERM

Think about the job you have for a moment. How has it changed?

Perhaps you are being asked to do more, better and faster, at less cost? (I hear those answers a lot.) It's safe to say the workplace has changed and will continue on that path. The needs and expectations of your customers will change. Your products and services will change. Your competitors will change. You will change too.

What you are able to do will change. Your circumstances will change. Perhaps more important than all of that is this realization: *what you want and need from your work is certainly subject to change!*

The "rules" for employees to be successful, secure, and satisfied are shifting at mind-blowing speeds. Sadly, many employees don't know they are playing on a new field, in a new game, with new guidelines:

- Job security is long gone. A new mind-set for success is required. You are more like an independent agent, marketing your capabilities, experiences, and results.

- You simply cannot wait for opportunity to present itself. The new workplace will ask you to create opportunity by increasing your contribution—by becoming more valuable.

- Technology has created an "always on call" mentality. It will be more important than ever to manage the boundaries between life and work.

- The skills needed for success will continue to evolve. There really is a stale date on your skill set, and it is quickly approaching. (Whoops, one of your skills just expired.)

- The workforce is mobile and virtual. (You may be surprised by who is competing with you for the job you have or the one you want.)

- Workplaces will continue to "move" at hyper speed. That means you will have to be crystal clear about your purpose, your passion, and your path.

- The resources you need to be successful may come from outside the walls of your organization in the form of mentors and thought leaders.

- Your peers and colleagues aren't limited to the people who work for the same organization you do; your personal and professional network will be more important than ever before.

That's a whole lot of moving parts! As I look at that list, I am energized! This is an amazing time to be in the workforce.

If you are waking up to the realization that you want more from your job than just a paycheck, welcome! This is a marvelous journey, brimming with potential, and you can make yourself indispensable and more employable right now.

GOOD NEWS! THE WORKFORCE IS DISENGAGED

I have good news for you. It's not as hard as you might imagine to stand out in the sea of people we call the "workforce."

Even more good news: As you stand out, you will deliver real value and create even more opportunity for yourself. As you add value and create opportunity, you will be energized, engaged, and fulfilled. (That's a whole lot of good news!)

To some degree the workforce is disengaged. In fact, a recent Gallup Poll survey measuring employee engagement revealed that 17 percent of employees are disengaged, 54 percent are not engaged, and only 29 percent are truly engaged. The workforce is filled with people who are not seeing or responding to the signs.[3]

Every day they bring heads and hands to work but leave hearts and souls at the door. For any number of reasons they *choose* not to fully engage. For many of these people the job is more like jail, and they are doing really hard time. For them life begins when the "whistle blows."

I call these people the "just mets," because they do just enough to meet the requirements—nothing more and nothing less. "They are wheelbarrow people," a manager answered recently in a leadership workshop. "Think about it! You can load them up; they have great utility, but if you don't push them, they are relatively useless." How's that for an analogy?

The secret is in how you apply your "discretionary" performance. Think for a moment about your discretionary income, what is left after the bills are paid. This is money you make choices with. You decide whether to spend it, save it, or invest it. As with our discretionary income, the decisions we make with discretionary performance shape our future!

The discretionary part of performance is what we do after job requirements have been met. It's the choice we make to add value, press through obstacles, and produce solutions. *Leaders long for the key that will unlock that kind of commitment from employees, and that is the key to becoming indispensable!*

Discretionary performance isn't just about going the extra mile—you aren't a workhorse, trudging along in your job. It's not even about working harder. It's about being more resilient and resourceful—connecting to the real priorities of the business you're in. Discretionary performance sets you apart, and it makes your job more interesting.

THERE IS A MORE REWARDING WAY TO LIVE AND WORK!

Why do employees disengage? Why do they disconnect and hold the best pieces of themselves back? To answer those questions, let's flip them over and solve them in reverse. What do people need to be fully engaged at work?

For authentic engagement I think we need four things: perspective, leadership, resources, and capabilities. At the intersection of these elements we will find our high-performance zone. If any of these are weak or missing, we slip a gear or blow a tire. Careers don't move very well on flat tires and blown engines.

CREATE YOUR ZONE OF HIGH PERFORMANCE*

I am fascinated by the number of people who still are waiting for these pieces to magically appear! When the organizations they work for fail to provide them, they become disillusioned and somehow feel betrayed. This may be a good time for a public service announcement.

---

* Graphic by Mark Hennick, Plum Design; www.plumspot.com

PUBLIC SERVICE ANNOUNCEMENT

We are all responsible for building, demonstrating, negotiating, and promoting high-performance factors at work!

Here's an interesting question: What would you do differently if you honestly believed these four elements were entirely up to you?

Let's take a closer look at each of them from that point of view, assuming they are a personal responsibility. They will not be delivered on a pretty platter, and they will not be included in your employee kit.

Develop and demonstrate perspective

Repeat after me (with feeling), "Performance isn't enough!"

Regardless of where we work, just knowing and doing our job won't create tangible, enduring value. We must understand the business and articulate how we personally impact it. We need to see and personally connect with the vision of the organization; we must understand how our work influences the bigger picture. All of this is known as alignment. When we are well aligned, we move better.

"Engagement happens when an organization gives a committed workforce 'line of sight,' a clear view of what they need to do to succeed in their daily jobs—the actions they take and choices they make—to help their organization achieve success."[4]

Something marvelous happens when we understand the strategy of the organization and connect with it. Our assignments have greater purpose, and we can articulate our impact. We are very clear about the difference we make, and others can see it too.

The question is: Do we see it? Is the connection clear?

To test the presence of perspective, I often use a "lifeline" exercise in leadership workshops. It's a little edgy and a bit risky. (Honestly, that makes me love it even more.)

Leaders hold their breath just a bit as I randomly call an employee (who is at work) on a speakerphone. I ask this employee to tell me what they do for the organization. Almost always I hear job titles and tasks. Rarely—almost never—do I hear about purpose and strategy and connection.

That's important because when people don't make those connections, they perform differently. They are working out of context. They prioritize and decide differently; the work doesn't resonate at a personal level.

You may work for someone who is a great "connector." These leaders know how to link every person in every position with the big picture. They carry the vision and push it through the veins of the organization. (If this describes your boss, send him a thank-you note or take her to lunch! That is real leadership. If that doesn't sound like the person you work for, alas, the connection really is up to you.)

You must search for opportunities to develop and demonstrate perspective. Here are six steps you can take to find the dots and draw the lines for yourself:

1. Become genuinely and insatiably curious about the strategy of the organization. Curiosity is compelling. Step out of your employee shoes for a moment; pretend you are an investor, a customer, a competitor, or a job candidate. Research the organization from those perspectives.

   What does the strategy look like from the outside, looking in? What does this organization care about? What are the vision and the mission? What is the difference this company intends to make, and how do they intend to make that happen? Beyond the walls of your department, what are the long-term goals and targets?

2. Practice making the connection. When you receive assignments and projects, think about how they impact organizational goals and priorities. How do your assignments affect time, money, or quality? What is the difference you will make by completing this task? How are you personally helping the organization step closer to its vision? How are you drawing upon your strengths and talents to make a real contribution?

3. Play the "So What, Who Cares" game. I love playing this game with live audiences. It is eye opening for sure. In my experience, most people struggle to articulate how they touch the big picture. They are comfortable talking about what they do on a daily basis, but they have trouble making the strategic connection.

   Here's how the game works: Choose one of your more routine tasks. We'll use filing as a simple example. Are you ready?

   Why do you file?

   You might say, "So our records are organized."

   To that I'd respond, "So what, your records are impeccably organized. Who cares?"

   Your answer might be, "Well…if we aren't organized, we can't locate important information."

   "OK. Big deal, you can locate really, really important information. SO WHAT! Big deal." (By now you may be a little exasperated. Play anyway. We are almost there.)

You could respond, "If we can't locate important information, we can't answer customer inquiries in a timely way."

Now we may be getting somewhere! Here's the connection: you are not mindlessly filing paper; you are making the organization more responsive and customer-centric!

I encourage you to talk about the work you do differently. Talk less about "the what" of it, and talk more about "the why" of it. When you do that, you are not only thinking about your work differently, *but you are also packaging it in perspective.* You make your value more obvious.

4. Ask and keep asking. If you can't find the connection between what you are doing and the big picture, ask better questions. Invite clarity with questions like: What are the top priorities, and how do I personally affect them? I love questions like this because they eliminate expectation gaps. (It really is quite possible to work very hard on the wrong things! That may sound crazy, but it happens all the time.)

If you want to push the envelope, you might ask, "What could I do to have a greater impact on the bottom line and the big picture?" With this question you are asking for opportunities to grow in your role. You are assuming (and rightly so) that you can make a bigger difference right where you are.

5. Consult your mentor. Review your job description with a mentor. Discuss the impact of your job and how you can demonstrate greater perspective. This is especially important if you work for someone who is not good at making the connections or helping you find them.

6. Create context! What do you love working on? What comes naturally to you—like breathing? Challenge yourself to incorporate more of that into your current role. This is another great opportunity to seek wise counsel. Bring a list of your responsibilities and an inventory of your strengths. Like puzzle pieces, lay them out on the table and look for new ways to connect who you are with what you do.

Demonstrate personal leadership

Right now, as you read these words, you may be working in a leadership vacuum. If that is true, you aren't receiving the direction, coaching, feedback, and support you need to be satisfied and successful. That is extremely frustrating, but the real danger is in waiting for leadership to suddenly materialize. Trust me when I say, "It won't."

I cannot tell you the number of times I've heard these words at the conclusion of a workshop or conference: "Oh, my boss really should have been here. He is the one who needed to hear this message!" Another variation (usually accompanied by a heavy sigh and rolling of the eyes) is, "This kind of thing really needs to come from the top. If management doesn't buy in first, all of these good ideas won't take off. I can't get off the ground with my action plan if my manager isn't on board."

To this I usually respond with a heavy sigh of my own and a public service announcement.

PUBLIC SERVICE ANNOUNCEMENT

Our personal effectiveness cannot depend on the
effectiveness of another human being or an organization.

The truth is that organizations can be very dysfunctional places. Our challenge is to be effective even when the people around (or above) us are not. Certainly, implementing new ideas is more challenging when we work with or for people who are not reaching for improvement or are open to change. If that becomes our excuse, we've lost the battle. Even worse, we've become part of the problem.

Hopefully you work for strong leaders with amazing vision that empower and equip you for success. If you don't, you are not excused from the table. You must fill that leadership vacuum. That's called personal leadership, and it looks like initiative, proactivity, and accountability. Personal leadership is modeling the right behaviors, walking in complete integrity, and owning your "stuff."

One way of managing a leadership gap is to clearly define it—specifically, what is missing and how that is impacting your ability to get results. These definitions will help you separate what is frustrating from what is mission critical.

Marcia found this "defining" exercise very helpful.

> I work for someone who is generally considered a weak leader; it really helped to isolate and prioritize the issues. Some things were just annoying. For example, my boss isn't good at giving recognition or acknowledging my work. That makes it more important for me to be self-motivated. I know the marketing message is up to me; I've found ways to reward myself and to make my results more obvious within the organization.

Other issues were derailing! The lack of leadership was literally blocking my progress. Our group lacked direction, and priorities were not clear. My manager is not strategically skilled, and that means I must be! I've concentrated on my own strategic agility, and I've learned to manage up. I ask the strategic questions, and I negotiate for the decisions and priorities that support the strategy.

Through this process of bridging the leadership gap, Marcia has grown tremendously. "It's actually been a very positive experience for me. The leadership vacuum pointed me right back to my own skills and capabilities. I stopped critiquing my leader and became a greater resource to him."

You may need to minimize a leadership gap with surrogates. Find your mentors and surround yourself with people who are empowered and have strong vision. I'll even underscore that last comment with this: *the weaker your leader is, the more important mentoring becomes.*

Manage your capabilities like the assets they are

Think strategically about your skills and capabilities, because what makes you successful today will not ensure your future success. You've probably heard some version of the saying, "What brought you here won't take you one step further." I'd add a little something to that. What brought you here won't keep you here! The workplace is constantly changing. That means what is expected from the workforce—from you—will also change.

We all have core competencies, which are the skills we own—our strengths. They are a natural part of how we work. With focus and practice, these abilities have become part of your "DNA." You may not even notice these strengths as such. For you, these abilities are like breathing; you don't have to think about them at all.

You also have skills you are working on. While you don't completely own them, they are emerging. With practice, these capabilities will shift to the strengths column of your life and work. The key here is to be more intentional in managing your development. You may need to negotiate for opportunities to explore and demonstrate the skills you want to own.

Finally, we have areas needing attention and development. These aren't just weaknesses or flaws in temperament! Quite often they are the result of new requirements and expectations. As we reach for more, more will be expected.

In chapter 18 of my book *Ready, Set... Grow!* you will find a balance sheet exercise or skills inventory. This audit asks you to acknowledge your strengths, emerging capabilities, and areas needing development. You are an asset to the organization; as you manage your skills, you increase your value. I encourage you to complete the inventory and review it frequently![5]

A skills inventory helps you recognize how you are growing and developing. It answers these questions: What are you learning, and how are you making your new skills more visible? What do you need to learn to become a greater resource? How are you making yourself top of mind for the right projects, assignments, and opportunities?

You can explore this concept more strategically by thinking about your job in fast-forward. Imagine your job five years from today:

1. Who are your customers?

2. What does the technology look like?

3. Who are your competitors?

4. What is different about your role?

5. What is expected from you?

You can also reach back in time. What questions do you wish you had asked yourself five years ago? Ask those questions now! Here are three examples from my own collection:

1. What will be most important to my customers?

2. What channels will I use to reach my customers?

3. How can I increase my capacity—my ability to deliver greater value to more people?

These questions are as relevant now as the first time I asked them. The answers change from year to year, but the questions have never failed to show me something new.

Managing your capabilities will certainly require a personal investment. Your investment may be time, energy, money, and almost certainly your comfort zone.

I get a little crazy when women who are carrying the latest designer bag and wearing amazing shoes tell me they can't afford a book, a coach, or a course! I love bags and shoes too, and there is nothing wrong with looking fabulous with all the right gear.

We need to invest in ourselves too—from the inside out. Beyond what your employer offers and provides in terms of training and development, you are worth a personal investment, and frankly, you can't manage capabilities without making one.

Negotiate for the resources you need

We must negotiate for the resources we need to be successful. Resources include success factors like time, money, information, tools—even people. Here's an example of negotiating for information as a tool for success.

The majority of employees I meet in conferences tell me they have a performance review scheduled once a year. This is information about performance—your performance! We wait patiently (and sometimes with great dread) for another person to tell us how we are doing. Worse than that, they are telling us how we "did" when it is too late to "do" anything about it. Let's look at how ridiculous that really is using football as an analogy.

What if football players didn't know what the score was until after the game was over? Imagine the game for a moment if only the coaches and referees knew the score. How would that change the dynamics of the game? How would it impact the players' performance?

The same thing can happen to us when we don't have access to the information we need to monitor our performance. When measurements aren't clear and agreed upon, when progress isn't visible—we don't know if we are winning or losing the performance game.

In this example, information or feedback is a success tool. Like any other resource, we may need to negotiate for what we need and manage it. Megan would wholeheartedly agree.

"For the longest time, I operated on the no-news-is-good-news theory," she told me. "That changed with a disappointing performance appraisal. Apparently no news wasn't good at all! My boss was just saving his feedback for that very special day. I promised myself that would never happen again, and I keep my word by asking for feedback on a regular basis."

Remember, when it comes to feedback, people give us what they have, not necessarily what we need. In my book *Ready, Set...Grow!* you will find the story of Connie, who changed the scope of her performance conversations by coaching her coach.[6] Like Megan, Connie learned that feedback was not something her boss was comfortable (or good at) giving. Connie negotiated for the feedback she needed by asking her boss specific, performance-oriented questions in real time. She uses questions to negotiate for the information she needs.

I encourage you to stop right now and think about what you need to be more successful in your current role. You may discover some of what you need is well within your control or at the very least your influence. An example of that might be more productive working relationships. Perhaps your efforts are blocked today by conflict and resistance. You certainly don't control how others behave, but you do control your approaches and responses. You initiate this "negotiation" by fine-tuning your communications and inviting your business partners to "play nicely."

Sometimes what you need isn't up to you; you have to ask for it. This might include stretch assignments, support, or even authority.

Recently a young woman in a mentoring program at work told me she was not able to complete her action plan because the team was shorthanded and her boss could not allow her to attend the required training. I asked her how she intended to negotiate for the time resources needed. Her face went blank.

It hadn't dawned on her to think about options and alternatives and to partner with her boss to create a solution. Even though her boss had recommended her for the program, when he told her she couldn't go, she simply accepted his decision, assuming she wouldn't be able to honor her commitment. She didn't see this as a negotiation, so she didn't treat it like one.

I hope these examples will help you identify your needs and plan to negotiate for them. (Remember, everything is negotiable!) If you aren't sure how to ask for what you need, consider the counsel of a mentor. Bring your "wish list" and work with your mentor to develop a negotiation strategy.

THE FOUR ELEMENTS ARE LIKE WHEELS ON A CAR—YOU NEED ALL OF THEM

These elements are connected; they work together. Like wheels on car, if you are missing one of them, you are in for a really rough ride! Imagine your car riding on two or three wheels! If any are weak or absent from your work experience, the others will be impaired.

If I don't have perspective, for example, I will struggle to be resourceful! How can I solve problems and be innovative if I don't understand the vision?

The point to all of this is really about our own power and responsibility. We can't wait for the organizations we work for to be brilliant, leaders to lead, and visions to inspire us! We must find ways to get connected and fully engage! When you look at really successful people in any job, you will find they have taken personal responsibility for that.

Here's the secret: you are self-employed, a private contractor, and a free agent! (We all are, and when we get that straight in our minds, marvelous things will begin to happen.) Many employees are passively waiting for their employer to develop them or for opportunities to present themselves. Flip it over!

You are a package of skills, capabilities, experiences, and results. Regardless of where you work or whom you work for, this package is what you "sell." It is the product you bring to market. It is your promise to deliver.

Your product has more than one version too! The original version is 1.0. As you add experience and understanding, and as you gain unique insight and even wisdom, you have a new version to offer. Frequent updating is recommended!

Consider our character Zoe for a moment. She was certainly lacking perspective! She saw her job as mindless and repetitious and unimportant. That frame most certainly impacted her ability to demonstrate leadership, and it obstructed her view of capabilities and resources. She whizzed past more than one moving sign without adjusting her course. Zoe lacks a strategy for her future; she is traveling without a map or a compass and with very little sense of direction.

GET YOUR MOVE ON!

Set aside time this week to evaluate your high-performance zone. In what ways are you relying on others to supply what you need to be successful? What can you do to enlarge the zone and release a new version of you?

Pray for wisdom and vision! That is a prayer God loves to answer.

Zoe spent the next two days wandering around her apartment in a shocked stupor. She needed to find a job—any job—very soon, but she didn't even know where to begin. She had finally succeeded in finding a sorry-looking copy of her résumé. It hadn't been updated since she'd been hired. (She'd thrown it together for her interview and hadn't needed it afterward.) "That was fair," she had reasoned with herself. "People with jobs don't need résumés."

The third morning of her "unplanned hiatus" found Zoe drinking very strong coffee and surfing the newspaper and Internet for jobs. She felt her confidence fading and her eyes crossing. This was overwhelming. Other than part-time jobs in school, she'd only had one real job, and she had been introduced to that position by a family friend. "I didn't even have to look for that job," she mused. "It just sort of appeared out of nowhere."

That was an interesting thought, and she spent the next few minutes realizing that is exactly where her last job has taken her. Absolutely NOWHERE.

She hadn't told her parents about the death of her job and was cleverly avoiding calls from Madeline, her best friend. Come to think of it, she hadn't told anyone. It was humiliating. Just how do you explain losing a "loser job"? Mother would worry, and Madeline would lecture—Maddy knew everything about everything. She didn't have the energy for that.

Around noon, panic arrived, and she spent the thirty minutes picking at her lunch and entertaining horrific thoughts of living on the street with Minnie, her cat. (On cue the selfish creature sauntered through the kitchen, apparently unaffected by their impending doom.)

After a miserable lunch date with panic, the mail arrived. There was just one envelope. The note was brief—handwritten on elegant, personalized stationery.

> *Zoe,*
>
> *You are at a crossroads, and you have more options than you might imagine. Call me if you are interested in making the very most of this moment.*
>
> *Alena*

Alena!

Zoe was astonished to hear from her. Alena was a marketing executive at the firm—a very powerful woman. Zoe had worked with Alena on several projects.

The projects were important, but Zoe's role had been mostly organizing meeting rooms, copying handouts, and bundling "mission critical" presentations. Why was Alena contacting her now?

A sarcastic voice whispered in her ear, "Maybe she needs a fresh cup of coffee."

No. That wasn't fair. Alena had always been very kind. "She noticed me. She talked to me and asked my opinion about things," she scolded herself aloud. "And I absolutely will call her!"

Zoe did make the call, and a day later she was sitting in a quiet corner of a coffeehouse waiting for Alena to arrive. The invitation for coffee was both a relief and a stress. Alena was always so confident and graceful. Just thinking about that made Zoe feel lumpish in the oversized chair.

The chair actually seemed to be swallowing her. She shifted awkwardly, nearly spilling her coffee. As she was mentally "shrinking" another full size, Alena appeared. Gaping up at her, Zoe could only imagine how ridiculous she must look at this very moment. If she noticed Zoe's predicament, Alena did not show it. When she smiled and said, "I am so glad you called," Zoe believed her.

They talked for a few minutes before Alena refocused the conversation with the awkward question Zoe had been bracing herself for: "How are you, Zoe?"

She had rehearsed the answer to this! The speech was supposed to sound something like, "I am doing well. Thank you. I'm taking a little time off to sort through my prospects." But in that moment with Alena looking her directly in the eye, she couldn't pull it off.

The teleprompter in her head went blank, and Zoe simply said, "I'm completely stunned and a little lost."

Alena smiled then—a broad, beautiful smile. "Well, then, we better get started. What are your plans at this point?"

Zoe winced as she thought, "Plans (as in plural, meaning more than one)? Are you kidding me! I don't have plans; I have panic attacks." Instead Zoe gathered herself and said, "I'm looking for a new position."

"What kind of work are you looking for?" Alena asked.

Zoe wanted to say, "The kind that pays the bills." Instead she mumbled some cliché about finding a challenging position with opportunities to advance.

Alena smiled. "What does that mean exactly?"

Her bluff had been called. Zoe felt herself sinking lower in this bottomless pit of a chair. "Honestly, Alena, I don't know what it means. It's just one of those handy little phrases. I've just been looking for openings I might be qualified for."

An image of the game babies play flashed in her head, and she saw herself as a giant square peg trying to slide into a round hole. No matter how she pulled and tugged, she did not fit.

Thankfully Alena rescued her just then. "There is nothing wrong with surveying the landscape. It works best if you have some idea of where you would like to end up—what you would love to do and become."

Zoe was getting frustrated now. "I'd love to dream about a dream job, but honestly I just need work. I just want to *become* employed."

"I understand," Alena reassured her. "As you search for a job, maybe a dream will find you. The best jobs are often found by word-of-mouth. Building your professional network will be an important part of your search. There's a women's networking event on Thursday. It will be a good opportunity for you to meet women from many different organizations. I'd like you to come as my guest."

Zoe had never attended a networking event, and she wasn't exactly sure how one goes about "building a professional network." Even so, she found herself nodding and agreeing to go. It certainly couldn't hurt.

They had finished their coffees, and Zoe could feel the meeting was coming to an end. Alena reached for her bag. "It's nice to be in touch, and I'd like to help if I can. Between now and Thursday, I encourage you to consider three questions: One, what is the real value you bring to an organization? Two, what is unique and special about you? Three, what is the most important lesson you have learned in the last ninety days?"

Alena opened the door and held it for Zoe. As she walked through it, Zoe had a question of her own. "Why are you doing this? I mean, why are you helping me? I know how busy you are and this," Zoe pointed to herself, "is a big project!"

Alena smiled. "Soon, I suspect you will answer that question for yourself. See you on Thursday, my friend."

Zoe watched her "friend" go. Nothing had been settled at all, but she felt a calm settle over her. Something had happened here. She wasn't entirely sure what it was, but she felt entirely different. She drove home thinking about the three questions.

two

STRATEGIC MOVES

Developing a Personal Strategy for Success

For the next day and a half, the three questions haunted Zoe. She wasn't used to thinking about herself or her work in this way, and she was struggling to understand the point of this exercise. To be very honest, the questions irritated her.

"The value I bring is doing my job every day with little or no drama," she grumbled. "I am not feeling particularly unique or special right now, and the lesson I just learned is brutal—without warning you can find yourself jobless. If that happens, you will be in a great big time-out until you can correctly answer three stupid questions."

She was in the kitchen again fussing over her résumé and thinking about ways to mass produce it. The calm she had experienced with Alena had slipped away, replaced by a more familiar sense of panic. Even so, she found herself searching the résumé to answer the three questions.

Slowly, at first, a list began to emerge. "I am good at organizing and coordinating. I am reliable and dependable and professional." She looked at the words she had scribbled on the page in front of her and came to the most horrible conclusion: "I am absolutely, completely boring!" With that she couldn't bear to think about special qualities anymore, so she returned with her bright red pen to the classifieds.

On Thursday afternoon, Zoe fought an overwhelming urge to call Alena to cancel her networking debut. She prayed there would be no answer so she could leave a well-rehearsed voice mail. She stopped dialing when she remembered how encouraged she had felt after their coffee date and how genuinely interested Alena had been. Abandoning her plan to cancel the networking date, she returned to the three questions, determined to find three answers (she couldn't imagine facing Alena without them): *What is the real value I bring to an organization?*

Then it struck her! The answer wasn't to be found in the value she had delivered in her last position. It was the value she'd left on the table. What could she have done to make herself more valuable—more of a resource to the organization?

Her mind began to replay meetings, presentations, and assignments. She had simply followed instructions: set up the room...test the equipment...distribute the agendas...check, check, check.

Seeing her role as basic and routine had invited her to work that way. That mind-set encouraged her to work blindly on tasks, checking off the list, without understanding the purpose behind what she was doing.

She hadn't even bothered to understand what was happening in those meetings—who would be in the room or the goals that brought them there! All of this added up to one important realization. She hadn't found ways to be remarkable or to increase her contribution.

There was a lump in her throat, but the answer was taking shape now.

The real value I bring to an organization is my ability to find the purpose or the strategy behind the tasks. That understanding allows me to innovate, anticipate, and initiate!

With the answer right in front of her, Zoe could not believe she had missed it before. She had been an order-taker, like a bored short-order cook in a country café serving up the daily special. Certainly there had been opportunities to impact the menu or the meal presentation!

As she checked boring tasks off the list day in and out, she had missed opportunities to be on the team! Energized now, she moved to the second question: *What is unique and special about me?*

Zoe thought about the images that popped effortlessly into her head. She was good at using metaphors and finding the "theme" of a project or presentation. "I know how to manage a message and connect people to the story with a metaphor. I am also good at planning and thinking ahead of the step I'm on. I can see the future," she informed Minnie.

Now she was getting it! She could feel herself making the turn as she faced the third question: *What is the most important lesson I have learned in the last ninety days?*

This one was easy. "I have learned that I am responsible for creating value. Assignments are simply opportunities to demonstrate greater capabilities. I don't always control what I am working on, but I do control my contribution. I've learned the level of contribution will ultimately determine what I am working on!"

Zoe sat back in her chair and somehow felt a little taller—slightly more powerful. "That's exactly what Alena had in mind," she told Minnie. "Alena is very good at helping people find their own answers."

As she dressed for the networking event, Zoe thought about how Alena had used questions to empower her. Initially Zoe had expected and wanted Alena to give her advice, to tell her what to do and how to fix this mess! Instead Alena had given her questions. She was excited to tell Alena what she had discovered.

She felt more powerful...until she walked through the door of the hotel banquet room. As if on cue, her confidence fled and self-consciousness locked arms with her.

She felt completely out of place here. All of these women had jobs, and from the looks of them, really important jobs. They were successful and confident and dynamic. She imagined herself walking through the room with a gigantic sign pasted on her back that read, "Unemployed Loser, Posing as a Successful Woman." (That image was so disturbing, she actually reached around just to make sure it really wasn't there!)

Sometimes the gift of a vivid imagination was not such a positive force, she decided. She shook her head to scatter the picture; that reminded her of the Etch

A Sketch toy that children played with. That picture made her smile.

Suddenly Alena was there, welcoming Zoe as if she were the guest of honor. "I am so glad to see you, Zoe. I've saved a seat for you next to me." Zoe followed Alena through the room as she greeted dozens of people by name. "You know all of these women?" she asked in amazement.

"Most of them," Alena replied. "They are extraordinary women. I hope you will get to know them too. Networking is about building relationships—understanding what people are working on and the challenges they're facing. Most of all, networking is searching for ways to help others succeed. You may have or be the answer someone in this room is looking for."

Zoe's heart fell two stories. She could not imagine having the answer for anyone here. She wondered if she needed to remind Alena of her "employment problem." Before she could respond, however, they were seated, and Alena introduced her to the other women at the table. "This is Zoe. We've worked together in the past, and I've been looking forward to introducing her to you."

That was amazing. Without missing a beat Alena had introduced her to each of the women at the table, and they seemed genuinely interested in her!

The big test came when Zoe was asked, "What are you working on?" Somehow she knew the right answer wasn't, "I am working on becoming employed." Thankfully her response appeared just in time, "I am focusing on building my professional network, and I am so happy to meet each of you."

THE TIME TO PREPARE FOR YOUR NEXT STEP IS RIGHT NOW—GET IN FRONT OF THE OPPORTUNITY CURVE

When a position opens and is publicly "posted," you can be fairly certain the hiring manager already has someone in mind. Before the next exciting project launches, the team has probably been picked (or at the very least, names have been tossed around). When great jobs hit the classifieds, professional networks are already in play. Phones are ringing, e-mails have been sent, and introductions have been made.

All of this means we can be the very best resource and arrive too late! We have to get in front of the opportunity curve.

PUBLIC SERVICE ANNOUNCEMENT

> The time to make your name top of mind and first in line for that job or prime assignment is right now.

I often meet people who are terribly disappointed in the way things have turned out for them professionally. They haven't received the promotion, recognition or opportunity they feel they deserve.

Feeling trapped and sidelined, they constantly scour job listings, searching for a better position. When these hopes don't materialize, they become more discouraged with the current situation. It's a frustrating cycle and very hard on one's self-esteem and confidence, equally hard on performance and results.

"I was so unhappy in my job. I started applying for anything and everything around the company," admits a young woman at a career-building conference. "I threw my name in the hat for positions I didn't understand or qualify for. I wasn't sure what I wanted

40

to do, but I was very clear on what I didn't want to do—my current job!"

The problem with this strategy is that it lacks a strategy! Throwing lots of applications at the wall doesn't guarantee something will stick, and there's another problem with it too: you risk making yourself appear irrelevant for the right position by saturating the system with "wild throws."

Even if you land a new position, it may not bring you to a new place. I've heard more than one "out-of-the-frying-pan-and-into-the-fire" story from women who just wanted out of their current situation. A few months into a new position they realize it's not an improvement, the grass isn't greener over here, and the wonderful people they now work with aren't perfect.

My best advice is to look for the answers where you are and where you wish to be. Use your current position as a place of preparation, not a place of frustration! (In chapter 3 you will learn how to reinvent the job you have to get the one you want! No skipping ahead!)

If you decide to make a career move, make it in the context of where you want to go—reach for something rather than run from something. (And if you are a casualty of downsizing and cost cutting, these tools will help you formulate a plan to get back on the path.)

In this chapter, you have the opportunity to design a road map for your career—one that is unique, customized to fit your dreams and goals. Think about that for just a moment, and let it sink in! You can design the experience you want to create. That's pretty powerful. I hope you will accept the challenge and explore these opportunity-mapping tools.

Paths Are Personal Things! Map Your Opportunity

Career paths are another example of how we sometimes wait for the company we work for to "give us the tool." (Incidentally, organizations really struggle with providing "career paths" for employees. There are so many variations that a one-size plan definitely does not fit all.) I cannot give you a map, but I can introduce you to the tools and processes that will allow you to create a customized path.

In researching this book, I explored marvelous tools for mapping your route. These include assessments, creative thinking tools, and even storyboards to capture your vision and make it plain. The processes you choose and how you put them together will create a map that is uniquely your own.

As you investigate these tools, you will learn more about yourself: what energizes and exhausts you, what inspires and motivates, and what you are naturally inclined to or "built for." When you deeply understand these things about yourself, you can take deliberate, intentional steps in your career. (No more wild pitches!)

You will literally invite the experiences that are relevant and real for you. You will find ways to make yourself top of mind for exciting projects and positions. All of this begins with clarity and self-awareness. Let's get started.

Discover your Camelot.

A favorite activity of mine is called Kings, Queens, and Fairy Tales.[1] This is a creative way to gather data for your strategy; it is often very energizing and revealing. This may be a very good first step as you begin to think about where you are and where you like to go.

To discover your Camelot, imagine your career is a kingdom. Like all good kingdoms, there are kings and queens, dungeons

42

and dragons, trouble and celebration. Perhaps you'll even throw in a knight or two.

Write a tale about the condition this kingdom (also known as your career) finds itself in today. The story must reflect kingdom (career) truths. Include strengths and weaknesses, opportunities and threats. Develop your characters and enjoy the process!

Your story will have a unique plot and its own cast of characters. As it unfolds, aspirations and frustrations may surface. Sometimes obstacles and fears are easier to spot in the lines of a story; solutions are often more obvious too.

Once you have finished your tale, write down three hopes for your kingdom. How would you like your story to be different? How do you want it to end? Of course, these "wishes" are up to you. For each of the hopes or dreams, determine what you can do to make them true.

This is also a great activity for teams and families. You might be surprised at the themes you see emerging from the stories. If you take the time, I imagine you will also be amazed at how much influence you have over the plot and how marvelous the story can turn out.

Use Mind Maps to explore your possibilities.

I am a long-time fan of Mind Maps. They are a brilliant way to shake up your brain, think more creatively, and arrange your ideas. You can use them to study, develop outlines, take notes, organize your thoughts, brainstorm, solve problems, and so much more.

Tony Buzan invented Mind Maps in the 1960s, and he continues to provide us with fabulous thinking tools. "A Mind Map is a powerful graphic technique which provides a universal key to unlock the potential of the brain. It harnesses the full range of cortical skills—word, image, number, logic, rhythm, color and spatial awareness—in a single, uniquely powerful manner. In so doing, it gives you the freedom to roam the infinite expanses of your brain. The Mind Map can be applied to every aspect of life where improved learning and clearer thinking will enhance human performance."[2]

Mind Maps begin with a centralized idea, and thoughts radiate from there. Here is a sample illustrating the laws of mind mapping.*

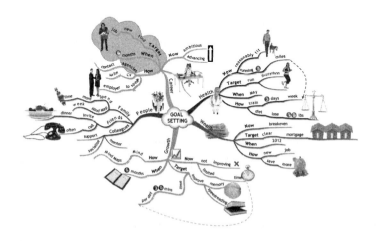

Get your story on the board.

Storyboards are another wonderful way to explore your vision and purpose. They are also excellent branding exercises for individuals, companies, and teams. Think of a storyboard like a photo montage or collage. Using words and images, you create a picture of your future. For me, storyboards are a graphic way to "record the vision and inscribe it on tablets, that the one who reads it may run" (Habakkuk 2:2).

Storyboards can be created with scissors and glue or on your computer using graphic design elements. Your board doesn't have to be one-dimensional! You can paste your images to any shape or form and call it decoupage with vision! Whatever the format, it is

---

* Tony Buzan is the inventor of Mind Maps. Permission to reproduce granted by The Buzan Organisation.

cutting and pasting, blending and designing. (Even if you are not artistically inclined, I urge you to give this a whirl! It's also a great family exercise.)

A powerful purpose makes all the difference.

Debi Blacklidge is a graphic designer with an extraordinary vision. When she first shared it with me, I was inspired and moved. It captured me! I found myself wanting to get involved and thinking of ways I could help make this dream come true. (That, by the way, is the true test of a vision: it energizes and motivates. It captures the imagination and gets people on board!)

Debi and her husband, Robert, share a love for horses. They have personally experienced the therapeutic, healing properties horses are known for. They also have a heart for children who have been neglected and abused.

Their vision is to bring horses that have been neglected and abused together with children who have been neglected and abused in a sanctuary situation—horses healing children and children healing horses. That is an amazing dream.

This vision ignites Debi and Robert. The work they do (also known as day jobs) fuels the dream. This is a perfect example of working in complete context and perfect alignment. "Now" is more meaningful and motivating with "then" in mind. The vision inspires even the day-to-day routines of life.*

Make no mistake about it; you are telling a story with your life and your work. Storyboarding is a marvelous way to capture your vision and bring it into focus. I approach exercises like this prayerfully, because I believe we are all born with great purpose. We are here to do something marvelous. I don't want to miss my appointment with the purpose God has for my life. I want to accomplish that purpose with absolute excellence.

---

* Storyboard by Debi Blacklidge, Dallas, Texas.

You can get very creative with this tool. One family makes storyboarding a tradition. Each year around the holidays, as they prepare for the new year, family members acknowledge progress and cast their visions with storyboards. The boards include achievements, memorable moments, and goals for the new year. The storyboards hang in a hallway of their home—they are absolutely beautiful. A walk down that hallway is both celebration and inspiration!

Use self-assessments and inventories to raise self-awareness.

A big piece of exploring your options is to understand yourself more. Who you are is a very important part of this process! It may be the most important part. You don't want to find yourself in a position that "cramps your toes" like a pair of shoes that don't fit properly. Toe scrunching is not recommended for shoes or jobs. Fit matters.

There are hundreds of tools and assessments available to you. You can literally get lost in the noise of it. Here, I'll introduce you to a few of my favorites and encourage you to make self-exploration one of your primary steps. This is certainly not an all-inclusive list, but these exercises will get you started and thinking about

others you might like to include. You can visit my Web site www
.dondiscumaci.com for links and more information.

1. Discover your talents and develop strategies for
   applying your strengths with Tom Rath's book
   StrengthsFinder 2.0. I like this resource because all too
   often we spend our time focusing on our shortcomings rather than developing our talents and strengths.

   The book includes access codes for online tests
   and downloadable tools. There is even a Strengths-
   Explorer for children.[3]

2. The Johari Window model is a simple and useful
   tool for improving self-awareness. The model was
   developed by American psychologists Joseph Luft
   and Harry Ingham in the 1950s while researching
   group dynamics. It is still widely used and can be a
   very useful exercise.[4]

   I recommend it as one way to explore perceptions
   and perspectives, gather feedback, and analyze your
   personal brand. (Without exception, when I introduce this exercise to a live audience, they love it. It
   generates a lot of interest and, quite often, great big
   "aha" moments.) That has been true for me as well.
   Each time I use the Johari, I learn something about
   my brand and about how I perceive myself and how
   others see me.

   If you look into the Johari Window and decide to
   give it a go, you can take an online test and invite
   feedback from others by visiting http://kevan.org/
   johari.

3. The most important story is the one you write. I am
   a hearty advocate of journaling. If you are not in

the habit of journaling or haven't journaled before, I encourage you to begin now. Capture your challenges and achievements, lessons and ambitions. Write, scribble, doodle, and draw. Before you know it, themes will emerge; you will make important discoveries.

My journals are simple moleskin notebooks; I carry one with me at all times. I use it to capture inspirations and observations. There is nothing fancy about the book, but the inside is filled with ideas that make me better.

4. Consider personality inventories and career assessments to learn more about your preferences, strengths, and interests. These exercises offer important clues about how you like to work, what you need, and what might trip you up.

A few of my personal favorites are the DISC Profile and iMapMyCareer.com. Assessments like these are fun and interesting, but the real benefit comes when you intentionally put what you have learned about yourself in action, using that information to manage yourself, your relationships, and opportunities more effectively.

Find and fill the gaps.

A gap analysis simply compares where you are with where you would like to be. After exploring some of the other tools, a gap analysis can help you pull it all together, create focus, and build momentum.

Complete your analysis by describing in vivid detail your current career reality. Next, envision your future job—the one you want. Forget titles here, and think about what you are working on and the difference you are making. This should ignite and excite. If it doesn't, keep going until it does.

I recommend thinking longer term, three to five years from now. The difference or gap between those two points becomes your action plan. This is not a "check-the-box" exercise. It is the difference between living a life by design or one by default.

The example below will help you get started. Remember, even though the action plan is in the middle, it is the last step. Think of it as the bridge between "here and there." Build your bridge by asking, "What must I do to prepare for possibility?" These are the steps that will make you top of mind for the opportunities you are looking for!

REALITY	ACTION PLAN	FUTURE POSITION
What are your primary responsibilities?	Education: workshops, courses, degrees, and certifications	What are you working on?
What skills do you rely on most to succeed in your current position?	Experience and experiences	What is expected of you in this position?
What do you love about your job?	Books, articles, and research	What experience and skills have you acquired?
What do you like least about it?	Identify mentors, experts, and associations	What is the difference you are making?
What are you known for?	Identify mastermind groups	How are your strengths applied?
What are you earning?	Special projects and assignments	What are you known for?
What are you learning?	Branding exercises	What are you earning?

REALITY	ACTION PLAN	FUTURE POSITION
What is most challenging?	Networking	What is most rewarding about the work you are doing now?
What is most rewarding?	Gather feedback	Who are your peers and colleagues?

Organizations do this work at a high level. They call it succession planning, and while companies have unique approaches and processes for "building a bridge to the future," there are some cues we can borrow from them to build our own bridges. Consider these points as you create your action plan:

1. Breadth of experience is highly valued. What can you do to demonstrate a broader perspective? Lateral moves, international experiences, job rotations, and special projects may be worth investigating.

2. Personal initiative is an expectation. Companies increasingly expect employees to own and manage their development plans. How will you demonstrate that initiative with your action plan?

3. Core values are often defined in behavioral terms. Many organizations have clearly defined success competencies. They've mapped the skills expected at each level of the organization. Look for ways to align your development with these indicators of success.

I encourage you to explore the career-pathing process in your company. In addition to the work you are doing on your own, take advantage of what is already in place. Raise your hand, ask the questions, and get plugged into the plan for your organization.

Once you've explored the possibilities and created a map, the journey begins. No aimless career wandering for you! Your energies will be more focused and fulfilling. Knowing where you are going will help you craft a clear, consistent message. That message begins with a look at your résumé and your online footprint.

HEADS UP! YOUR RÉSUMÉ IS BECOMING OBSOLETE... RIGHT BEFORE YOUR EYES!

I have often said (with great gusto), "Dust off your résumé, people! Keep it up-to-date, and while you're at it, keep it with you at all times! It isn't a résumé; it's a marketing brochure!" That has been good advice for a time, but perhaps not for much longer. This calls for an updated public service announcement.

PUBLIC SERVICE ANNOUNCEMENT

Your résumé is racing toward obsolescence.

Some predict traditional résumés will be extinct within five years.[5] The clock is ticking even as you read this! Good news! If your résumé is buried somewhere in a box, stored on a floppy disk, or saved on your old laptop—you won't have to worry about it too much longer.

Employers and prospective employees are changing the way they interact with each other. More and more people are job-seeking online. That means employers are inundated with hundreds, even thousands of résumés, and that begins to look a whole lot like SPAM! It's very hard to stand out in a crowd of electronic files, but managing the "virtual you" is exactly what you must do!

The new résumé will be electronic, and the formats are already

51

taking standard shapes—LinkedIn, Facebook, Internet search engines, and...hold on tight...your personal blog, video blogs, and even YouTube video posts. When I mention this in presentations, reactions range from "a pin could drop" to a unified "uh oh."

You've probably heard sayings like, "It's easier to borrow money when you don't need it," and "The best time to find a job is when you have one." That wisdom holds true here as well. Building your online presence is definitely a well you want to dig before you are thirsty. (If you feel like you are running behind the curve on this, don't spend one more minute scolding yourself with could haves and should haves.) Here's what you can do about that starting today:

1. Spend some time thinking about your "online" branding strategy. That's not as daunting as it might sound. Strategy is simply thinking in "fast-forward"—six months, one year, or five years from today. What do you want people to think, feel, and believe about you? What do you want them to know and understand about you? How will you make that impression using the latest tools and technologies?

2. Strategies resonate when they are unique. That might mean doing something no one else is doing, or it might be doing something others do but *differently*. Stop reading for a moment and make a list. What is your uniqueness? What sets you apart from others in your field of interest?

3. Remember, you are a rich collection of skills and experiences. How will you showcase those to attract the opportunities you want? Remember you aren't

looking for a job; you are looking for a threshold. (Thresholds are also known as brinks, as in the brink of your big dream.)

Think Like a Real Estate Agent and a Marketer—Get Your Name Above the Fold!

In graphic design "above the fold" refers to location. In a newspaper, stories above the fold take priority and get more attention. You also have a story to tell, and you are competing for a priority position…online. When prospective employers search for you (and they will), will your name be above the fold? (That is prime real estate!)

Do an online search of your name. How many "hits" do you get? Where are they, and what are they? Use these tips to position or reposition yourself above the fold.

1. **Build your online profile.** Again, you'll want to consider social networking utilities like Twitter, LinkedIn, Plaxo, and Facebook. All of these forums invite you to "present" yourself. They are marvelous branding exercises. I recommend you choose a few and focus your energy to get real traction. This is time-consuming stuff, so be selective and consistent in creating your online footprint.

2. **Refresh frequently!** The utilities listed above give you an opportunity to "declare" what you are working on. This may require a shift in the way you think about what you are doing. The real news is what you are learning, how you are growing, and the difference you are making. Instead of posting, "I am sitting in customer service training," you may want

to declare, "I am learning new ways to partner with my customers."

3. **Write articles to establish yourself as an expert in your field.** Consider writing an article for your organization's newsletter, or even contribute to an industry publication. Blogs are simply articles posted online. Successful blogs are well followed and become dynamic forums for discussion. The authors of these blogs are branded as thought leaders, and they deliver real value. There is a wealth of information out there about how to start and sustain a blog. You can be up and running very quickly. Before launching, make sure you have developed a strategy for your blog.

4. **Read and comment on other people's blogs.** This is a fabulous way to test the water before diving in. Read and weigh in on topics that interest you. This is also a great networking strategy. As you comment on articles in your field of interest, you will find yourself dialoguing with experts.

5. **Reach beyond yourself.** A great way to get your name above the fold is to give your time and talent to the causes you care about. Get involved in your community and partner with your organization. Volunteer to make a real difference, and talk about what those experiences have meant to you and for you.

Résumés and your online presence are just a few examples of how things are constantly changing. That will always be true. The tools and devices you use to market yourself now will serve you for a time. These will also "morph" and evolve. There is no finish line when it comes to managing your brand and marketing your value.

The key to all of this is consistency. It's better to do a few (positioning) things with regularity than to attempt everything sporadically. Market yourself like a marathon runner—in it for the long haul—rather than a sprinter dashing for the finish line. Pace yourself!

GET YOUR STRATEGY ON!

At any point in time, you should be ready to answer this question, "What is your strategy?"

Honestly, there is nothing mystical about being strategic. People throw the *strategy* word around a lot. What it really means is looking forward, finding a way to do something no one else is doing, or do something others are doing in a different way.[6]

I hope you will take the time to formulate your strategy, perhaps choosing some of the tools presented here. Be patient with yourself and with the process. In my experience, the process is just as important as the result you seek. Many people tell me the journey was far more precious than the arrival. What you discover about yourself and your possibility just might astonish you.

GET YOUR MOVE ON!

This week I encourage you to explore your story. What pieces of your story are working well? Which parts are not? How satisfied are you with the plot and the characters? How do you want your story to turn out?

Remember, you are the author and the publisher. You can erase and edit, underscore and highlight. There will never be another story like yours. Like you, it is one of a kind. Find your story, and learn how to tell it well.

Zoe enjoyed the rest of the evening. For a little while she almost forgot about her big employment problem.

The agenda included a guest speaker, an update on a benefit for women, and plenty of time to meet and get to know each other. The conversation at her table was lively. Somehow the topic turned to "lessons learned the hard way," and the stories resonated with Zoe.

"I am still learning this tough lesson," admitted Alison, the owner of a small advertising agency. "I take on things that don't belong to me and find myself resenting others for not doing their part." She laughed then and said, "I actually invite people to take advantage of me, and then I resent them for it!"

Zoe found this curious. How could this woman who was so professional and "all together" be encouraging others to take advantage of her?

"Here's a perfect example," Alison continued. "Last week my team went on a field trip. We thought it was time to stir up the creative juices by breaking routine and getting out of the office. We decided on a day at the zoo." She leaned forward then and said, "I was proud of the idea and feeling very good about my management style." With that she sat back in her chair and smiled. Clearly there was more to this story.

"It was a long walking tour, and I came completely prepared with this giant bag. Honestly, it's huge and bright red. When we left the office, there was barely anything in the bag; it was nearly empty. But as the day rolled on, 'things' were added to the bag." Alison emphasized the word *things* by lowering her voice and raising an eyebrow.

After a dramatic pause she continued, "When a team member needed a place for her camera, I opened the bag. Someone else bought a stuffed animal souvenir for his son—into the bag it went. All day this went on. Before long the bag was completely full and very heavy! The strap of it was digging into my shoulder, and my neck was aching. Picture me now schlepping through the zoo with this giant neon-red burden!"

Alison underscored the word *burden* and threw herself back in the chair as if entirely exhausted. She was a wonderful storyteller!

"I was so absolutely irritated! I was falling behind the group, grumbling to myself, 'Why do I *always* end up carrying everyone else's junk around!' The farther we walked, the grumpier I became. Then it dawned on me. I was carrying this load because I'd made myself available for it! I brought the big red bag. And that's not the end of it; I do this at home and work too.

"I carry around an invisible bag and invite others to drop their junk inside. I end up packing what they should be or could be carrying. Now I've realized, when I do that, I actually rob others of the contribution they could be making. I am stealing the achievement that belongs to them."

The other women at the table laughed with Alison; clearly they could relate to this "Tale of the Big Red Bag." Zoe enjoyed the story too, but what struck her most was the ease with which Alison was telling it. She made self-discovery look simple and painless; that made it possible for the others to share their own challenges and issues. They were actually enjoying this game of show-and-tell!

This was all foreign to Zoe. She worked very hard to conceal her shortcomings. She was actually good at hiding them even from herself!

Zoe had walked into this place with her "success face" lacquered on like a mask. It was designed to protect her from the penetrating stares of truly successful women (all of whom would see right through her if the mask fell for a nanosecond).

As these wonderful women shared their lessons learned, she felt the mask slip just a bit. She actually reached up to straighten it. (That almost made her laugh aloud, and the mask nearly fell off.)

Zoe thought of her own hard lesson and the three answers she would share with Alena. It is exciting when the flash of discovery comes. In that moment you see so clearly what has been holding you back, and then you realize you have the power to make a change!

That's when she remembered her resolution to take initiative, to find ways to be on the team and add real value. Perhaps her lesson wasn't reserved for a job. Maybe there was an opportunity to make a real contribution right here. Pulling up her resolve, Zoe made the leap.

"I love that story," she said. "And I love your original idea of breaking out of the office in search of creativity—like a safari—searching for the next great idea. It's brilliant, and you did make a discovery. It was self-discovery." That was the easy part. What she planned to say next required a new level of boldness. "What would happen if you shared the 'big-red-bag' story with your team?"

There was an ominous pause at the table. All of the women were looking at her now, and she felt uneasy. Her mask had flown off; there was no retrieving it now. Perhaps she had gone too far by making the suggestion.

Then Alison said, "What a great metaphor for what we were trying to accomplish. It was a safari, and there certainly was discovery. I hadn't even thought about sharing what I learned with the group." Alison thought for a moment and made a decision. "I am going to do that! At our next team meeting, I am bringing the big red bag!" Now she looked directly at Zoe and smiled, "Next time we are all together, I'll give you an update."

Zoe felt something beyond relief. It was acceptance, a sense of belonging, and feeling valuable all rolled up into one emotion. She returned Alison's smile. "I will look forward to the sequel. You may be surprised by what others discovered on the safari. Telling your story may give them permission to tell theirs; that may be the whole point after all. Perhaps it isn't about hunting for creativity. It's finding what blocks and destroys the creative flow."

"That's profound, Zoe, and it reminds me of something I read in the newspaper some time ago." Cindy, who had been quiet until now, was leaning forward with keen interest. "We do block the flow, and we also have real perception problems. There was a very interesting social experiment performed in Washington DC. It literally was a performance.

"A very nondescript man in jeans, a baseball cap, and T-shirt stationed himself next to a trash can during morning rush hour in a busy train station. He played six classical pieces on a violin.

"People pressed by on their way to work. No one knew this, but the violinist was Joshua Bell, one of the greatest musicians in the world. He played some of the most complex pieces ever composed on a violin worth $3.5 million dollars!

"Some people stopped for a moment, sensing something special, but they did not linger to take it in. They were on the clock, pressed for time, rushing to meet the day.

"The point of the experiment was: Do we perceive value out of context? Do we notice what is special and unique and brilliant, or do we miss it in the mad rush of life? This man sells out performance halls around the world, for heaven's sake, and in forty-three minutes he only collected thirty-two dollars and seventeen cents!

"It's interesting though, that the article talks about children being drawn to the performance. Somehow the kids sensed it. They knew it was something special. They seemed to be saying, 'We should stop.' But the parents pushed them on!"[7]

Cindy sat back in her chair and the other women seemed to be taking in the story. It was Alena who spoke next. "What else are we missing?" She paused for a moment and said, "It's the out-of-context part that connects with me most," she mused. "People weren't expecting a world-class musician to be playing intricate pieces on a Stradivarius violin standing next to a garbage can! When things are out of context, we risk missing them entirely."

"The children sensed it," Alison reminded the group. "There is something important about that aspect of the story."

Zoe saw that too. "That is important. Children look at things differently, and that allows them to see. That's why going to the zoo was such a brilliant idea; it was a deliberate shift in perspective."

The group talked a little more about perspective, creativity, and living in context. The conversation was thought provoking, and Zoe found herself thinking about what she could have done differently in her last position. She had missed it, like the people who passed the concert violinist in the train station! The opportunity contained within her job had been out of context for her. She had passed it by without seeing what was special about it and possible in it.

For just a moment regret perched on her shoulder and whispered horrible things in her ear. She didn't allow that for long. Zoe shook her head and straightened her shoulders. Regret lost footing and bounced right off. Zoe imagined her regret landing with a thud under the table. She smiled at that and kicked her foot just a bit.

As the agenda came to a close, business cards were exchanged along with promises to call soon or have lunch. Zoe didn't have a card to offer, but she accepted several. She even joined a working committee for the women's benefit. This was a team of seven women charged with publicizing the event and securing corporate sponsors.

As she was signing up for that commitment, Zoe overheard a group of women planning a mastermind meeting. She had no idea what that was all about but planned to ask Alena later. It sounded interesting.

Zoe had enjoyed the evening very much and was already looking forward to the next month's event. As she and Alena walked to their cars, Zoe said, "Thank you for inviting me tonight and for asking the three questions. Would you like to know the answers now?"

Alena just smiled. "The answers aren't for me, Zoe; they are for you."

INSIDE MOVES

Moving Sideways (or Backward) to Get Ahead

Zoe went to bed thinking about her first ever networking event. She felt like she had made an important turn somehow, but without a road map, she was unsure of the destination and how to get there. Even so, as she drifted off to sleep, she was for the first time thinking about what she would love to do instead of just finding a job.

Three answers swirled in her head, and she dreamed about a safari.

Morning found her at the kitchen table again. Instead of studying classified ads, she was writing notes to each of the women she had met at the networking event. She had just finished the last "so nice to meet you" when the phone rang. It was Alena.

"Good morning, Zoe," she said. "I am walking into a meeting, so I have just a moment or two. Alison phoned this morning. Her team is starting a large project next week. Her resources will be stretched beyond thin, and she is looking for some help. If it's a good fit, would you be interested in a temporary assignment?"

The line was silent for a moment while Zoe took it in. She genuinely liked Alison, and the idea of working with her was exciting. The word *temporary* was running through her mind, and then she remembered one of her answers: Find a way to contribute. Be on the team. Make the most of your opportunity. "I'd love to discuss it with her!" she heard herself say.

"Wonderful!" Alena said. They said quick good-byes and agreed to meet for coffee that afternoon.

Zoe glanced at the sorry-looking résumé. It was not a reflection of who she was, what she was capable of, or what she was looking for. It didn't invite a second look or communicate what she valued. She wadded it up and tossed it up in the air. Out of nowhere Minnie scrambled across the floor to bat it around. "Sometimes," she informed the cat, "you don't revise. You reinvent."

Reinvention began with a visioning exercise. Zoe imagined herself fully engaged—contributing at a whole new level. Words and images began popping into her mind: *collaboration, calibration, synergy, creativity,* and *community.* She pictured a sparkling river, stopped and jammed by logs and debris. Each of the logs represented an obstacle or a problem, and the still water was becoming stagnant and sour. She could see the resources needed to break through: *shared vision, problem solving, communication, resiliency,* and *innovation.*

She flipped open her laptop, and the images came together on a storyboard. It was fantastic! Working on it energized her, and the thought of working like this was electrifying!

When she glanced at the clock, she gasped. Where had the day gone? It was nearly two thirty; she didn't want to keep Alena waiting. She quickly saved the storyboard, grabbed her laptop and keys, and made a dash for the door. She laughed on the way out. Minnie had fallen asleep, clutching the crumpled résumé. "You can have it, Minnie. I won't need that version of myself anymore."

Thirty minutes later Zoe walked through the door of the bistro and stopped short. It looked different somehow. The chairs were smaller; when she sat across from Alena, she didn't sink to the point of disappearing. She almost laughed aloud when she realized the chairs had not been replaced. She was the difference! Barely able to contain her excitements she blurted out, "Alena, I am so glad you are here. I have something to show you!"

After showing Alena the storyboard, Zoe sat back in her chair and said, "This reflects the way I want to work, the difference I want to make, and the reputation I intend to build. It relies less on my experience and more on my experiences."

Alena smiled. "What exactly does that mean? What is the difference between your experience and your experiences?"

Zoe hoped she could articulate her meaning. "Experience is where I've worked and what I've worked on—job responsibilities, titles, work history, and so on. Experiences are what I have learned, the difference I've made, and how I've leveraged opportunity and challenge to create enduring value. I don't have a great deal of experience at…well, anything. When it comes to my experiences, I can tell a compelling story. I can use images and metaphors to make my story more interesting and memorable."

Alena placed her coffee cup on the table between them and leaned forward, clasping her hands. She looked squarely into Zoe's eyes. "You do tell a compelling story. It is fabulous. How do you plan to 'publish' it?"

Taking a deep breath, Zoe continued, "I am learning that we are all responsible for our experiences and for maximizing and *creating* them. In addition to a traditional résumé, I intend to build an online presence. I am going to get my name on the top of the list, or 'above the fold,' by building my online profile. I may even consider writing a blog. I've been following several blogs recently, and they are good ways to build credibility and community.

"I am also going to connect with a cause. This will allow me to create more experiences, deepen my professional network, and make a real difference. The women's benefit will be a good start. I am excited about the goal of helping women enter or reenter the workforce." Zoe realized she was now thinking aloud. Her next steps were pressing to the front of her mind, like horses at the paddock eager to run.

"You have a come a very long way in a few short days, Zoe," Alena smiled. "If the opportunity is right, I think you would be a wonderful resource to Alison on her next project. It is a big step for her team and, in her words, somewhat of a risk—it could make or break her. You made quite an impression on Alison. I've let her know you are interested in speaking with her about a temporary role."

Zoe was grateful. "Thank you for that, Alena, and for introducing me to your networking group. One thing is certain; if I am presented with the opportunity, I will find a way to make a valuable contribution. I could learn a great deal from Alison. In fact, I already have."

With the time remaining, they talked about the networking event. "I was surprised by how open everyone was. Challenges and mistakes are very personal things. Alison was so comfortable talking about her weakness," Zoe commented. "I admired her for that. I learned from her story, but I'm not sure if I am ready for that kind of disclosure."

"Self-disclosure is pretty powerful." Alena held up her hands and spread her fingers wide. "When we are open, we invite others to be the same." Then she intertwined her fingers. "At that moment connections are created and strengthened. There is an important distinction here. Alison did not expose a weakness. She shared a revelation. Those are very different things.

"There is a time, a place, and an audience for telling that kind of story. Perhaps we can err on both sides of the equation. We can fail to be open in the right moment, or we can make ourselves vulnerable in the wrong setting."

That made perfect sense to Zoe. "Openness is like a gift," she said. "We must be deliberate and intentional about whom we give it to, when, and where."

"Exactly!" Alena said. "That is a perfect analogy."

They rose to go, and Zoe thanked Alena for making time to meet with her. "Honestly, I couldn't wait to show you the storyboard. Thank you for your encouragement and interest. This has been a wild week, but I think I am finding my balance. Things seem to be falling into a good place. I couldn't have done it without you, and I am grateful. I am still wondering why you would do all of this for me. That's a mystery, but I want you to know how much I appreciate your help."

Alena just smiled. "It is good to see you too. You have the opportunity now to build a powerful brand and tell a compelling story. Let me know how it goes with Alison!"

That evening Zoe worked on her storyboard and thought more about her personal brand. What did she want to be known for? When people introduced her, what would she like them to say?

Her mind wandered back to the old job, and she couldn't help but think about that brand. She hadn't intentionally designed it, but in just a few months it had taken solid form. Every action and interaction reinforced it.

Words like *boring*, *repetitious*, and *tedious* floated around in her head. The words she had used to describe her job had ultimately branded her—*bored, apathetic,* and *dull.*

Zoe wanted to share these insights with Alena, but not because she could change what had happened. That wasn't the point. She wasn't even beating herself up over missing the opportunity and being fired. She did want to explore what could have been. It was like a personal case study; Zoe needed to extract something of value from the experience.

REINVENT THE JOB YOU HAVE TO GET THE JOB YOU WANT

Do you believe in reinvention? How would you go about reinventing your job? As you read the following stories of women who did exactly that, look for the steps and strategies they used. Each of the three stories is unique, but if you look closely, you will find common threads deliberately woven to create new possibilities.

CHANGE YOUR POSITION, NOT YOUR TITLE

A bank teller for two years, Carla was young, bright, and extremely frustrated. "I was interested in banking," she explains, "but I thought my career would move a little faster. After two years on the teller line, I wasn't even on the corporate radar. As I looked at the traditional career path for a teller, I became even more disillusioned.

"My career goals (mostly financial at the time) didn't match the company's plan for someone in my position. I wasn't exactly sure what I wanted to do, but I was convinced I was on the wrong track. The company didn't have a career plan that fit. Clearly it was up to me."

Carla met with several of her colleagues. These associates were loan officers, investment counselors, and relationship bankers. "At first I just wanted to find out more about their positions and how I could partner with them to refer business. That's when I fell in love with lending! I was fascinated by the process. It included things I love—analysis, negotiation, and problem solving. And," she smiles, "the pay scale was much better!"

Very quickly, Carla became number one in the company for teller referrals. "As a teller, I was in the perfect position to notice ways to serve a customer more completely. My business partners taught me what to look for and what make up the qualities of a good sales lead."

As the top referring teller, Carla was definitely on the radar now! "Management asked me to share my 'secret referral sauce,' and that gave me an opportunity to demonstrate my process and my understanding (and love) of lending. I made several presentations and developed a referral checklist for tellers."

In her company, tellers weren't eligible for credit training, but that didn't stop Carla. She bought a textbook on consumer lending and signed up for an evening tax preparation course; there she learned how to read tax returns. "The information is out there, if you are willing to go get it," Carla asserts. "I made myself eligible for the training I needed to achieve my goals!

"Something else happened too," she remembers. "Through this process I created a new group of peers! My business partners stopped seeing me as a teller; I became a colleague, a valuable resource. My title hadn't changed at that point, but I was in a new position."

Within a year, Carla was plucked off the teller line and placed in a credit-training program. "That had never happened before," she admits. "To my knowledge a teller had never been considered for the lending program. I was definitely an exception."

I would wholeheartedly agree. Carla is exceptional. Today she is managing a very successful credit team. As she tells her story,

Carla is mindful of others who might be feeling stuck or sidelined in their careers. "I reached out, and my colleagues reached back with the information, encouragement, and recognition I needed to reinvent my job. I look for opportunities to do that as well. When I see that spark of initiative in someone behind the scenes or on the line, I march right over and introduce myself."

CARVE OUT YOUR NICHE BY UNDERSTANDING WHAT PEOPLE NEED

Donna works for a large construction company and is responsible for entering data and distributing reports. She reinvented her job by understanding what her internal customers needed.

"The projects we manage are massive and complex. Sometimes they last for years," she explains. "My job is tracking the expenses and generating financial reports. What a revelation when I realized people are making really important decisions based on the information I provide!" She smiles broadly before moving on with her story. "For the longest time I didn't know how the reports were used or what information was most important to the project managers. I just punched the numbers in and printed the reports out."

Donna started asking questions and gathering feedback from her internal customers. Once she had a strong understanding of what people wanted and needed, she redesigned the reporting format and frequency of several reports.

"We were printing some reports daily that project managers really only needed to see once a week," she recalls. "There were three reports no one ever glanced at, and one report was so cumbersome and difficult to read it was virtually useless.

"I was shocked to learn that one project manager had given up on the corporate reports and built his own! He was spending hours in the evening creating the reports he and his team needed. We were able to incorporate some of the work he had already done in making the information more user-friendly and relevant, so it was a team effort. People really stepped up to make the changes successful."

This was a motivating initiative for Donna. As she puts it, "I love solving problems and improving processes. This was a real challenge, and it's made a real difference. The project managers are getting the information they need, when they need it, in a format they can really use. That makes them more successful. It was such a rewarding experience for me."

GET ON THE TEAM!

"I was so 'over' my job," Sue admits. "I felt there was nothing left to learn in my supervisory position. In other parts of the company, exciting things were going on—new technology, growth, and leading-edge projects. My department was business as usual. We felt like fans on the sideline, and we wanted to play in the game!

"I started by learning everything I could about the work going on in other departments and divisions. That was easy to do. My friends and colleagues were proud to share what they were working on. I was even invited to several project presentation meetings.

"I discovered two projects that would directly impact my group, but we hadn't been included in the process. I invited myself by demonstrating how input from my unit would benefit the project. We became a resource to the projects. Suddenly, my team was on the team and working with people around the organization on exciting initiatives."

As Sue is telling her story, I wonder how this would work for someone who isn't in a supervisory or management position. She has this to say: "Even though I am a supervisor, I have a manager too. I had to make sure my efforts to connect with other work teams were nonthreatening to my boss. I involved her in the process, and she supported me because I sold her first."

She goes on to say, "I think sometimes we give up too soon and tell ourselves, 'I can't make a difference because I'm not the boss.' Everyone in my organization has a boss; even the CEO is accountable to the board of directors and shareholders. We can't always wait for change to happen at the level above us. We can often turn our bosses into our champions."

Reinventing the job you have requires a new way of thinking about what you do and the value you bring to the organization. It also asks you to think differently about your colleagues and customers—who they are, what they need, and how you can make them more successful. It might even require you to think differently about what is possible for you!

Each of these stories reminds us that when we create value for the organization, we create opportunity for others and for ourselves. The four elements are certainly at work in these examples—perspective, leadership, capability, and resources. These women found their zone of high performance!

Personal initiative and networking are also common themes in these examples. All of the stories involve reaching out, often across the boundaries and borders of the organization, to forge business relationships. These women involved people in collaborative ways.

It is possible for you to reinvent the job you have. Sometimes those efforts will throw open doors of opportunity, and off you'll go! Or maybe moving out of your job isn't the point at all. It's about loving your job again. In either case, you've made a really good move.

SOMETIMES YOU HAVE TO TAKE A STEP BACK TO GET AHEAD

When does it make sense to step back in your career? By that I mean starting over, taking a salary cut, or "stepping down" on the organizational chart.

Tammy made that move when she realized that being a manager wasn't a role she wanted to play. "I always assumed that was the ultimate goal," she laughs. "You work really hard to get promoted. Then you manage people. That was the success model in my mind."

Tammy did work hard, and she was promoted. As a manager, she was miserable. "I absolutely hated it, but I didn't know what to do about that. I thought there was something wrong with me. For five excruciating years I worked in a job that didn't suit me at all. When I finally admitted to my boss how unhappy I was, she asked me to think about what I would like to do instead. What a concept!"

For Tammy getting ahead wasn't about money or titles. It was about job satisfaction and fit. She worked with her manager to find a position that she was truly suited for. On the organizational chart, that career move may have looked like a step down, but for Tammy it was stepping into a role she enjoyed.

Stepping back might also make sense if you are trying to "jump the track" in your career. That is, when you want to move from one discipline to another or from the staff to the line.

Staff positions support the line or revenue-producing roles. If you are staff, it can be very difficult to move to the line. That was certainly true for Dina, a mortgage loan processor.

Dina had been processing mortgage loans for several years and wanted to become a loan officer. (That is a classic example of jumping the track from staff to the line.)

As she tells her story, she remembers the frustration. "No one took me seriously. People reminded me that I didn't have sales experience, and at first I accepted that. Then I realized selling is really about relationship and service and negotiating. Good loan processors do all of that every single day!"

Dina became a mortgage loan assistant for six months to gain the experience she needed and to build her sales credibility. Her deep knowledge of the loan process served her well, and she quickly became a top-producing loan officer. "If you plan to jump the tracks, be prepared to talk about the skills you are bringing with you," she advises. "Your experiences are not irrelevant! They give you unique insights and perspectives."

Dina stepped back temporarily in her career to prove herself in the role she wanted to play. She would tell you it was more like backing up to take a run at the new opportunity.

In a game of strategy, lateral or even backward moves can make a great deal of sense. In the context of your strategy, don't be afraid to consider your alternatives. Give yourself permission to take a run at your opportunity.

GET YOUR MOVE ON!

Forget about titles and job descriptions for a moment. Find a way this week to increase your value by understanding your customers more, solving a problem, or building a new relationship at work. (I dare you.)

Enlarge your peer group and your opportunity by growing your perspective.

———————————————●———————————————

The next morning as Zoe poured her first cup of coffee, the phone rang. It was Alison, and Zoe tried to keep the relief out of her voice. She had wondered if the call

75

would really come, and that made her realize just how much she was counting on this opportunity.

Alison's voice was upbeat, but she came right to the point. "Good morning, Zoe. I know it's very short notice, but are you available later this morning? The team is meeting to discuss the new account, and I thought this might be a great way to introduce you to the group and a potential opportunity."

Zoe had managed to keep relief out of her voice but failed miserably hiding her excitement. "I'd love to meet your team!"

"Wonderful," Alison laughed. "The meeting starts at ten. I can e-mail you the address with directions. Will that work for you?"

"That works," Zoe said looking at the clock and calculating how much time she needed to get ready. "I'll be there. Thank you, Alison!"

When she arrived, Zoe was a little breathless, partly because she had rushed to be on time, but mostly because she was anxious about the meeting. She took a moment outside to gather herself and breathe before pushing the heavy door open. "It's not automatic," she thought. "It takes a little effort to open a new door, and that's just fine with me."

The lobby was small but beautifully decorated. Almost immediately a young woman stepped into the room and greeted her warmly. "You must be Zoe," she said, extending her hand. "I'm Sara. Alison is on the phone; she'll meet us in the conference room shortly. Come right this way."

Gathered in the conference room was the most eclectic, colorful group Zoe had ever seen! They were absolutely striking, and she could literally feel the energy. Sara introduced her to each member of the team, and Zoe made her way around the table to shake every hand. She felt welcome here and was instantly at ease.

Alison arrived then, and the meeting was quickly underway. "I've invited Zoe to join us this morning. She may be a good resource to the team." Alison took a deep breath before continuing, "And if we take on this account, we will need very good resources. We have a decision to make, and we need to make it quickly."

Zoe couldn't help but notice the word *if*, and her heart sank three stories. *If* they decided not to pursue the account, she wouldn't be needed even temporarily. She forced herself to focus.

"I am not going to make this decision for us," Alison informed the team. "I am going to tell you what I know, both the size of the opportunity and the size of the risk. This is something we must want very much, and it will cost us something."

From there Alison described the magnitude of the new account. "This client is larger than all of our other accounts combined. The opportunity is utterly amazing." Alison stopped and looked around the room. Every face was searching hers.

"This client is very powerful and demanding. We have this opportunity because their current agency has been a disappointment. If we take this on, we will have to expand our capabilities. We will have to grow into this account. That means working hard—very hard—for the next several months. We also need to consider what could happen if we grow to accommo-date this client only to lose the account. This could be the best thing that ever happened to us, or it could be devastating."

Next Alison gave everyone a folder. When the last one was placed in front of her, Zoe felt like a member of the team. This feeling was new to her and quite unexpected. She'd arrived as a visitor and was already experiencing a strong sense of belonging; this was unsettling because she didn't know what to do with that feeling. Did she even know how to be on a team? Was it possible she'd come this far in life (and work) without ever being on one? Impossible!

Her mind whirled, searching for team memories, and came up empty. "There's a team in here some-where," she thought, imagining herself rifling through old trunks and cartons in a dusty attic. The attic exca-vation was interrupted as Alison continued.

"This is all the information I have on the account and the client. It includes the contracts we are currently reviewing, some historical data, the research I've done, and the client's expectations and requirements."

Alison leaned forward then, and Zoe could see how deeply concerned she was. "I don't know if we can handle this account. Perhaps we aren't ready for it. I do know I can't take this on without you. I'm asking this team to decide whether or not this is a good move for the agency. If you determine it is not, I will respect your decision. If you choose to move forward, I'll need your plan for managing it."

As she stood, Alison turned to Zoe. "The team's discussion may be helpful to you as well, Zoe. It will give you a chance to learn more about the project. Depending on what the team decides, I'd like you to tell me how you might fit into the plan and the role you would play."

Before turning to go, Alison reached under her chair and placed a bright red bag on the table. "This decision belongs to you."

The team was silent for several minutes as they pored through the paperwork in front of them. Zoe was searching the folder too, but she didn't know for sure what she was looking at or for. She glanced at the red bag and remembered the lesson it carried. Alison must trust her team very much, Zoe thought.

Todd was the first to speak. "We've worked hard for an opportunity like this. It could put us on the radar or wipe us completely off the map."

The team worked for the next several hours without taking a break. The discussion was very animated and passionate, but it was focused too. These people were amazing. Even though Zoe was there to observe, it was hard not to jump into the discussion. She resisted the temptation and concentrated on taking fabulous notes.

She was shocked when Sara said, "Zoe, what do you think?"

The answer flew right out of her mouth, "I think you are some of the most talented people I've ever met. I also think you trust each other and Alison trusts you, and for good reason. If there is a team that can pull this off, it's probably this one. I know you'll make the right decision. Selfishly, I hope you go for it."

They were all looking at her now, and she wondered if she had overstepped. Who was she to offer an opinion about the group or this decision? Sara smiled then and said, "I hope we go for it too."

"Well, let's assume for a moment we are going for it," Todd suggested. "How would we do it?"

Back to work they went. The energy had shifted from debating the issue to solving the problem. It was exciting to see the plan fall into place.

When Zoe looked at the clock again, it was well after five o'clock. The day had disappeared and the decision was made. Zoe gathered her things and said good-bye.

"It has been a good day," Zoe thought as she drove home. She couldn't remember a workday going by so quickly—ever! "How weird is it that I felt like a real member of the team when I don't actually work there?" she asked the windshield.

Still, something was bothering her. Just out of reach, it was skirting the edge of her mind. "We're missing something," she told the windshield. For the rest of the drive, she tried to catch the thought, but it was too quick for her.

four

BAD MOVES

How to Paint Yourself Into a Corner and Other Lessons Learned the Hard Way

Zoe woke up early the next morning in a state of frustration. She wasn't sure exactly how or when to follow up with Alison. She didn't know when the team would be meeting with Alison to discuss their final decision, and she hadn't been able to corner the nagging thought.

"I know we are missing something," she told Minnie. "And I am not going to sit here and just wait for something to happen." She reached for the phone—as if on cue it rang in her hand.

That startled Zoe and she jumped, nearly dropping the phone. Minnie flew from the room in a dramatic show of feline fright. It was Alena.

"Good morning, Zoe. How are you?"

Zoe almost laughed when she said, "Excited. I met with Alison and her team yesterday. I could get used to working in a place with that kind of energy."

"They are a great group," Alena agreed. "I've worked with them on a couple of community projects. That is a very impressive team."

"Alena," Zoe said preparing to shift gears, "I have something to ask you. It's a lessons learned kind of question. To use a football analogy, it's Monday morning, and I'm watching my game tapes; I'd like another perspective about how I played."

Zoe shifted in her chair, but her discomfort was coming from the inside. No amount of fidgeting or rearranging would help, and it was too late to reconsider. She took a breath and continued, "If I could go back in time, there are many things I would change about the way I approached my job. I can't hit the rewind button, but I can fast-forward to the learning part."

Then she braced herself to ask the kind of question that leaves you wide open and vulnerable—the kind of question you can't take back (and when you hear the answer, you might really want to). "If you and I were watching the game tapes together, what advice would you give me about my performance?"

There was a pause on the line, and Zoe found that more than excruciating. When Alena answered, her voice was kind and confident, "I'm happy to offer feedback, Zoe. I'd rather do that in person. Are you free for lunch?"

They made quick plans to meet at noon, and the call ended.

Zoe spent the rest of the morning reviewing pages of notes from the team meeting. She used a Mind Map to capture the details and organize the ideas. The central idea was "Project Transformation." She chose that theme because the team had talked about how this account would transform the company and how they would have to grow in order to successfully manage it. As she worked, the map took the form of a tree with branches and roots and ultimately beautiful fruit.

One of the branches was empty. At the end of it was a large question mark, representing the thought still evading her. She knew it had something to do with her role and the part she would play in the transformation, but she didn't have the answer. She studied her storyboard and thought about the three questions Alena had originally asked:

1. What is the real value you bring to an organization?

2. What is unique and special about you?

3. What is the most important lesson you have learned in the last ninety days?

Perhaps the answer was inside of the questions.

When she walked out the door to meet Alena for lunch, all the branches of the tree were full and flourishing. She had found what she'd been searching for.

Zoe arrived a few minutes early, and now sitting alone in the restaurant, she felt uneasy. This was the first time in her life she'd ever asked for feedback. In her experience, feedback was something you endured, not something you invited. "This might sting a little," she admitted to herself. She picked up the menu and thought, "I'll be having the feedback sandwich with a side of humble pie."

That idea unleashed her mind, and for the next ten minutes she was brainstorming cuisine for a feedback menu. Soul-searching salad, sprinkled with bits of "what were you thinking?" A side of awareness, drizzled with reminders of your mistakes, and to start—an epicurean platter to sample your shortcomings. She was so involved in this crazy concoction she didn't even see Alena approaching.

They exchanged friendly hellos and nice to see yous.

It was Zoe who steered the conversation to the feedback she'd been bracing herself for. "I am trying very hard to understand what happened so I can make sure it never happens to me again," she said quietly. Suddenly, she felt very exposed and vulnerable. She imagined every eye in the place resting on her; she battled an urge to check.

"I admire your openness, Zoe. This has been a painful experience, but I suspect you will not regret it in the long run. Sometime in the future you might even say it was the best thing that has ever happened to you."

Alena paused to sweeten her ice tea. Stirring it she said, "Feedback is a brilliant tool. It's all around us if we'll pay attention. There's feedback in every interaction, in all of our results—successes and setbacks—even in our relationships. There's feedback on the inside too. If we can learn to be still and reflect, if we ask the right questions, and if we are willing to listen for truth, the answers will come." Then she asked, "What do you think happened to you?"

Zoe swallowed. "What I believed about my job became how I did my job. I thought of it as dull and boring and unimportant. Looking at it like that kept me from seeing the opportunity inside of it. I could have been a greater resource to the team. I could have been more curious and asked more questions and shown more initiative." Zoe sat back in her chair. "That's quite a list, and I'm just getting started."

"I think this experience has served you well then," Alena said as she held up her hands and opened her fingers. This was the signal of self-disclosure Zoe remembered—openness in the right time, the right place, with the right people.

Alena continued, "I did not lose a job, but I left one believing I'd been treated very badly. I viewed my boss as an adversary; seeing him as the enemy gave me permission to treat him like one.

"He was a tyrant in my mind—an arrogant, control-seeking, manipulative dictator. I got lost in the dysfunction of it and ultimately resigned. I have no doubt my days had been carefully numbered. He was patiently building a case for my termination, and I was giving him everything he needed to get the job done. I beat him to the punch by quitting. Ultimately, there were no winners." Alena paused for a moment, and Zoe knew this story was not an easy one to tell.

"For a long time after leaving I comforted myself with his flaws. I still remember where I was standing when truth looked me right in the eye. I was in the business section of a bookstore. I was casually flipping through a book on personal accountability when I suddenly realized nothing had happened to me. I'd fully participated in the game, and I'd cashed in my credibility to play."

Zoe didn't ask for details. She didn't need them to understand Alena had been caught up in a struggle for control and had removed herself from the game before losing it entirely. She did have a question. Quietly she asked, "It sounds like a very difficult situation. Looking back on it, what would you do differently?"

Alena smiled. "I'd grow up! I'd realize that my personal effectiveness cannot depend on the effectiveness of another person. I'd look for ways to be a business partner, to help my boss succeed and make controlling me absolutely unnecessary."

Zoe knew that Alena had just shared something very important with her. That was an honor, and she felt trusted. "Thank you for sharing your story," she said. "It's nice to know I'm not the only one having to grow up and take personal responsibility. I will say, it's hard for me to imagine you being anything less than brilliant at work."

Alena laughed. "Brilliant comes with a price."

Lightness returned to the table, and Alena went on, "The people I admire most in life have made some wrong turns and bad choices along the way. The difference is in how quickly they get it, take responsibility for it, and correct the course. All of their stories have a common thread: it is personal accountability, absolutely refusing to be or behave like a victim. I hear that theme in your story too, Zoe. You've made an important turn."

Zoe thought about that for a moment. "I hope you're right. I also hope I find a job soon!"

"I'm not worried about that at all," Alena said. "Your opportunities are ready for you. Until now, the question has been, are you ready for them?"

It wasn't until she was driving home that Zoe realized Alena had done it again! "She didn't give me answers; she asked the questions that helped me discover my own answers."

Six Really Good Ways to Derail Your Career

There are probably dozens of really good ways to derail yourself at work. Here I'll outline what I call the "big six." I'm betting you relate to at least a few of the "bad moves" described in this chapter, but the real message is that failure is not fatal, and setbacks need not be permanent. You can recover, rebrand, and move on. I do believe in reinvention!

Sometimes the setback becomes the most positive catalyst of all. That has certainly been true for me. Through the pain and disappointment you grow deeply, and you gain wisdom, understanding, and perspective. Even failure will serve you, if you will allow it.

As promised, here is short list of common missteps along with examples and strategies for course correction. As you read through these, look for the common themes of accountability, trust, and relationship.

1. Avoiding conflict

One of the most common issues I encounter in the workplace is conflict avoidance. Oh! How far out of our way we will go to sidestep the unpleasantness of conflict. If we aren't careful, these detours can take us completely off track. By feeding our fear of confrontation, we can lose our way entirely.

I've seen entire teams hopelessly derailed by avoiding conflict. Take, for example, a project team charged with improving a customer service process. As the group formed, it was all courtesy and charm; everyone was so nice and, in their words, "just thrilled to be on the team." Within a very short period of time, two strong personalities emerged, and the cracks began to show.

Project meetings were dominated by arguments between the outspoken two. Others hesitated to contribute, and several team members simply gave up trying to get a word in. "I just wanted to be done with it," Lisa recalls. "The meetings were horrible. Nothing was getting done; it was a total waste of time. I stopped caring about the project and did the bare minimum to get by. Honestly, I thought our solutions were off the mark, and I didn't believe our plan would work. When I tried to contribute, my ideas were discounted and thrown down. In the end, I endured the stupid meetings and did what the team asked me to do, but I wasn't buying any of it. Nothing remarkable happened as a result of our work."

This scenario perfectly follows a model Patrick Lencioni illustrates in his book *The Five Dysfunctions of a Team*. What begins as "artificial harmony" leads to a lack of commitment and low accountability.[1] It sounds something like this in your head: "I don't think we are on the right track, but I am not comfortable with the conflict, so I will nod and smile. I know this will never work, and when it doesn't, I will be right."

When you get right down to it, conflict really is a trust issue: "I don't trust you enough with my truth. Our relationship can't bear the weight of honesty and openness. We haven't learned to value each other in that way. If you disagree with me or don't do what I think you should do, the breach between us grows. Eventually the gap is too wide, and we can't span it."

I love this advice from consultant Geoff Crane: "On a team, when trust is breached, the focus shifts from results to the breach."[2] That is big wisdom! When trust is violated, the violation becomes what the team is thinking about, talking about, and defending against.

When you reframe conflict as an issue of trust, the solutions become more apparent. It's no longer about having your say and getting your way. You get to the root of it by building a relationship that invites (even requires) openness.

Mary can certainly relate to that. "I am very results oriented," she admits. "My problem with conflict was not avoidance at all; I was the person who bulldozes through. I'm the one teaching others to avoid conflict! When I learned how to balance my need for results with valuing relationships, conflict looked more like creative collaboration. I didn't need to force my ideas anymore. I learned how important it is to create buy-in by involving people more thoroughly in the solutions. We get to the answer faster, we enjoy the process more, and the results are better."

Think about a conflict occurring in your life or work now. How is avoidance exasperating the situation? What impact is it having on your relationships and results? How is it affecting you?

Diane told this story about a personal conflict at work.

"For years I've worked with one of my closest friends, but our relationship has suffered some wear and tear. My friend is very pushy, and I am very easily pushed. I never said anything because I didn't want to hurt her feelings. How do you tell someone you think she is overbearing and bossy? I found it easier to just avoid her or go along with her plans, but my resentment was building a thick wall between us."

Diane's avoidance didn't spare her friend's feelings after all. "I wasn't being honest," she told me quietly. "When I finally found the courage to say how I was feeling, she was stunned and hurt. She felt I had been less than honest with her, and that was fair. Because my friend is so direct and outspoken, she assumed others would be too. I've learned to set my boundaries with her—to say yes when I mean yes and no when I mean no. More than once, I've let her know that I am feeling 'swept downstream' by her take-charge approach. She gets that. We don't always agree, but our relationship is healthier."

To face conflict in a productive way, you must have your script ready! Be prepared to talk about what is happening and the impact it is having on you, on relationships, and on the results you seek.

Finally, plan to ask for what you need specifically. *Conflict is negotiation!* What are you asking for?

Here's how that script might sound for Diane in the example above: "Sometimes I feel pressured by your plans and opinions. That makes me uncomfortable, and it's damaging our relationship. When we are working together or making plans, I need you to ask more and tell less. Include me in the process of deciding."

Diane's story also makes another important point. If we allow it to, conflict will serve us. When we work through it effectively, we emerge with greater awareness, better solutions, and stronger relationships. Eliminating conflict is not the goal! It serves a valuable purpose in our lives.

You may need to practice your lines with a mentor, a mirror, or—taking a cue from Zoe—the windshield of your car. If conflict is difficult for you, rehearsals are strongly recommended. I can't guarantee you'll ever become comfortable with conflict. That isn't really the point. The key is to manage conflict so that it doesn't manage (or derail) you.

2. Runaway emotions

Lack of composure also belongs on the short list of bad moves. This one is tough because feelings are powerful, and it isn't easy to rein them in. When things don't go as planned, or when we are under a great deal of pressure, emotions can whip us around and tip us over. To make matters worse, when we feel like it the least, managing our emotions probably matters the most!

When we are angriest, most frightened, or most frustrated—when emotions are taking us over—we must seize control. The paradox is that we won't *feel* like doing that at all. Later when things calm down and we can think more clearly, we'll wish we had handled things differently. By then the damage is already done.

Rhonda supervises a customer service team, and composure is

a real problem for her. "I am a crier," she boldly announces. "I don't want to cry, and I try not to, but every time my boss has feedback for me, he sets a box of Kleenex on the table between us. He fully expects me to cry, and I haven't disappointed him yet." Rhonda's tears have become one of the most predictable elements of her brand!

"How do you keep your face from turning four shades of red when you're angry?" Brenda asks. "That is not a voluntarily reaction!"

Losing composure may look like crying or shaking or turning bright red in the face. Perhaps your throat tightens, turning your voice into a high-pitched silly squeak. Maybe you become sarcastic, short, or defensive in the heat of the moment. However it manifests, a lack of composure erodes credibility and steals your personal power.

PUBLIC SERVICE ANNOUNCEMENT

Make no mistake; if behavior becomes a pattern, it becomes the brand.

If composure is a problem for you, here are five good remedies:

1. The pitch of your voice is controlled by the amount of oxygen crossing the vocal cords. When you are under pressure and feel your throat tightening, breathe!

2. Become more aware of your emotional triggers. Use index cards to catalog the last twenty times you've lost composure. "Most people who have composure problems have three to five repeating triggers. Criticism. Loss of control. A certain kind of person. An

enemy. Being surprised. Spouse. Children. Money. Authority. Try to group 90 percent of the events into three to five categories."[3]

3. Once you've identified your patterns, think about why these scenarios are a problem for you. What is at stake? Do you fear embarrassment or failure? Are you afraid of being taken advantage of or losing control?

4. Awareness is a beginning, but ultimately you must prepare for more effective responses. Review your triggers, and think about your objectives in each of these scenarios. What do you want or need in these situations? What is the best course of action to achieve that goal?

5. Intentionally shift your focus from the emotional to the logical aspects of the situation. Instead of trying really hard not to cry or become angry, mentally list the facts, objectives, and steps to the goal.

Rhonda's trigger was criticism. Brenda's was feeling out of control. Both of these women worked hard to develop objective-based responses. They established goals for their emotionally charged situations and outlined the steps they would take to achieve those targets.

Rhonda also agreed to stop reinforcing a negative brand by declaring, "I'm a crier." She created a new declaration for herself: "I respond effectively and professionally to feedback." For a long time, her boss continued to place the tissues strategically between them at meetings, but she didn't need them. When the box discreetly disappeared, Rhonda knew her brand had been repaired.

3. Naïveté about office politics and grapevines

I've yet to find an organization without a grapevine or politics. Both of these are just givens. They do exist, and you must manage yourself in relationship to them. If you don't, eventually you will "step in something" that is both unpleasant and unproductive.

When it comes to politics and grapevines, my first recommendation is to intentionally develop your professional network. Understand where the power lives in your organization. Who are the gatekeepers and decision makers? Who has the information and the authority to make things happen? Who are your resources? What do these people need, and how can you help them?

This kind of awareness will also allow you to tailor your approach. One size does not fit every situation! There will be times when a direct approach is exactly right. In other situations, diplomacy will unlock the result you are looking for. The shortest distance to the goal may be confronting a problem head-on, but choosing that route may alienate the people you need to get the job done. You'll need more than one approach in your pocket. You'll also need wisdom to read the situation and choose the right strategy.

Unfortunately, not everyone will have your best interests at heart; you will encounter people at work who have less than positive intent. (It would be nice if our competitors worked for other companies, but sometimes they sit in the next cubicle.) I like this advice from author Robin Fisher Roffer: "The best defense against sabotage is to use your brand as a life raft. If you hold tight to your attributes you *will* sail beyond the saboteur's influence."[4]

Even when it comes to managing politics, your brand is a powerful tool. There's one more really good reason to spend time on that and get it right!

In chapter 10 of my book *Designed for Success*, you'll find "Twelve Rules of Engagement" and tips for breaking through the invisible boundaries between departments and work groups also known as "border problems" at work. Success looks like turning adversaries into allies, inviting your business partners to play nicely, building trust, and demonstrating complete integrity in your communications.[5]

Politics and grapevines make fabulous mentoring case studies! These are the situations mentoring is made for. Bring your story to a mentor, talk through the scenarios, practice reading the plots, and develop viable strategies for navigating these sensitive and potentially career-busting scenes.

4. Failure to act, decide, and accept responsibility

One of the worst moves is failing to! At work this looks like you are not resourceful, you don't trust yourself, or, even worse, you don't want to accept responsibility. Here are nine examples of failing to move. Brace yourself; some of these may look very familiar.

1. Seeing a problem and deciding it's not yours

2. Waiting for the information you need to do your job well instead of proactively searching for it

3. Asking questions you can find the answers to on your own

4. Missing opportunities to demonstrate more initiative—waiting to be asked rather than seeking new assignments

5. Needing to be led when you could be taking the lead

6. Giving up too quickly when encountering resistance or barriers

7. Using excuses to explain disappointing results or outlining problems rather than solutions

8. Focusing on things you cannot control (also known as whining)

9. Asking your boss to make decisions you should be making

As I look at this list, scenarios flip through my mind. One of the most ridiculous scenes is a receptionist reading a romance novel at the front desk of a large corporation. Apparently she has nothing else to do! (That just makes me want to say, "Are you kidding me?") If you are going to read a book at work, at least make sure it's something that will help you grow and became a greater resource to the organization!

Another scene involves an employee asking her boss how she should handle a business issue that is clearly within her responsibility. (Perhaps she is looking for reassurance or attention. Or maybe she doesn't want to own the result if it turns out badly.) She leaves with the answer, but a little piece of her professional credibility has been chipped away. She may not even notice the erosion until she is applying for a position with more responsibility (and pay). How can the organization trust her with more when she isn't fully functioning in her current role?

A third scenario comes quickly to mind; a new employee just spent half of her day waiting for others to train her. They are busy and she is brand-new. "They are so unorganized and unprepared for me! There was nothing for me to do," she complained. "So I just played games on my cell phone and texted my friends." Honk! Wrong answer! Being proactive means reaching for (not waiting for) what you need to be successful. While you are waiting to be trained, learn everything you can about the organization. This is when you pull a business book out of your bag or ask for the company newsletters or annual report to read.

What do you see when you look at the list above? What examples of failing to act, decide, or take responsibility have you seen or even experienced? What would you add to this discussion?

5. Overachievers and hamsters on the wheel

Remember, everything is negotiable. Right now in your workplace, negotiations are taking place. Sometimes we can miss the opportunity to negotiate because we don't view situations as negotiations!

Kate learned a valuable lesson about negotiation—the hard way.

Kate was facing an impossible deadline. To achieve the goal, she worked more than seventeen hours a day for a solid week. She was very successful moving that mountain, but now she has problem. Her boss was overheard in the hallway saying, "I really didn't think we'd make it. That was a tough deadline, but Kate really stepped up. Now I know what this team is really capable of."

When Kate heard this, she was very disheartened. She hadn't publicized the overtime, and she didn't mind pushing hard on the project. But instead of recognizing her all-out-no-matter-what-it-takes effort, her boss sees the potential for more aggressive deadlines! He is pleased with the outcome, but he doesn't understand what it took to make that result possible. Kate's "accommodation" has become a new "expectation" because she failed to set appropriate boundaries and negotiate.

"I fell into an overachiever's trap," Kate admits. "I saw the deadline as a challenge, but I failed to see it as a negotiation, and now I've created a monster! No one noticed the hours I worked to make that happen because I was the only one left in the building at midnight! Next time, instead of simply accepting the challenge, I am going to communicate what it will take and what I need to be successful. That includes more help and time off to recover and protect my life-work balance!"

Rachel learned that you must negotiate for the experience you need and make yourself "top of mind" for prime assignments and exciting projects. As a manager for a large media production company, her work is intense, technical, and deadline driven.

"I wanted to take on more complex projects and assignments," she admitted. "There is so much I wanted to learn; the technology and techniques are constantly changing. You can turn around and be out-of-date! The problem was that my plate was spilling over. I was so busy with day-to-day, routine tasks that I was missing out on the experiences I needed to refresh my skills and take them to the next level. I didn't dare ask my boss how I could be a greater resource. I was terrified he would answer and I'd leave with another assignment!"

Rachel was working "on the wheel." Like a hamster, she was running as fast as she could, and without a doubt she could make that wheel fly. She was doing excellent work, but it was the same work over and over again. To break the cycle and get off the wheel, Rachel needed to negotiate for new experiences. That meant negotiating to strategically add *and subtract* assignments.

"The specifics were important," she recalled "When I met with my boss to discuss my goals for development, I defined the experiences I needed. I showed him the responsibilities that were holding me back and asked for help aligning my assignments with my goals. I had to show him the benefits and what this would mean for the company and for our customers. It hasn't happened overnight, but I am slowly getting off the wheel. My tasks are more aligned, and my boss is very aware of what I need to grow."

High-performance success factors are woven through this negotiation. Rachel found her zone of high performance. She demonstrated personal *leadership* in analyzing her work and approaching her boss with a plan to increase her *capabilities*. She asked for *resources*—time and experience. She also understood that as a resource to the organization, she was underutilized by working on the wrong things. Finally, Rachel used *perspective* to present the benefits of her plan.

6. Down the documentation hole

I am honestly astonished by the rigorous game of documentation that takes place in many organizations. Sometimes I am amazed that any real work gets done with the furious need to capture and note every infraction and injustice!

Here are two variations of the game:

1. An employee receives negative feedback at her performance review. This infuriates her because it feels so unfair. In response she plans to document, document, document—everything she does. She also documents the shortcomings of her supervisor; for good measure she makes some interesting notes about her co-workers too. Her diary is filled with tantalizing tidbits as she manages to justify and explain her behaviors.

2. A supervisor is frustrated with an employee's performance. She begins to build her case with thorough documentation. She watches for every infraction and is not disappointed by the number of occurrences observed. Every day she makes her list and checks it twice.

In both of these scenes, the focus has shifted from strategy, productivity, and development to justification, explanation, retribution, and police work! Down the documentation hole we go!

What if that energy was invested in real communication? What if we placed a higher value on relationships and results? Here's a really scary question: *What if documentation wasn't an option? What would you do instead?*

At her last performance review, Susan's manager questioned her productivity and asked Susan to look for ways to increase her personal contribution. Susan left that meeting stomping mad, determined to "make her contribution more obvious." Her plan was to document everything she did…literally. From e-mail to phone calls to meetings, Susan kept a careful list. She was still keeping score when I met her at a professional conference.

As she described her plan, I'm quite certain my mouth dropped open. I pulled up a chair and sat down next to her. My initial response was a shocked, "Really? This is how you plan to prove your value to the organization?"

She blinked in surprise and said, "Yes. That is my plan. Apparently my supervisor doesn't think I do *anything*, so I am keeping track of *everything*."

We had a little chat about that, and before the workshop was over, she'd calmed down, grown up, and developed a more productive plan for demonstrating value and responding to the feedback. Her plan included a conversation with her manager communicating her disappointment with the negative perception and her desire to change that. I think the plan helped her feel more powerful and hopeful. I'm certain it put her on a more productive track.

Susan's predicament is not uncommon. Perhaps even the majority of employees don't get enough feedback or the right kind of feedback (and the dreaded annual performance review isn't cutting it). We must take charge of these performance conversations and manage feedback as a dynamic real-time business tool. Susan left the workshop determined to leverage feedback as a resource for success.

After it's all said and done, documentation does serve a purpose. (Human resources professionals are breathing a collective sigh of relief here.) I would challenge you, though: documentation may protect you, but it cannot become the alternative for real communication, conflict management, and human development. In my opinion we go to the documentation place too often and too quickly.

PUBLIC SERVICE ANNOUNCEMENT

When documentation becomes the focus, we've lost sight of the goal.

So there you have it—the "big six." Can you relate to them? Do they resonate with you?

The underlying message in this chapter is awareness. When you are aware of the career traps, there is no need to fall into one. If you have created a hole for yourself, learn from it and move on! If you are willing to take responsibility for the parts you own, you will emerge wiser and more prepared. The traps become launching pads, and off you go!

GET YOUR MOVE ON!

Traps are designed to ensnare and deceive. They can be tricky (the really good ones always are). Look for and recognize the traps that threaten your credibility, your brand, and ultimately your opportunity.

This week pay more attention to your actions and reactions. When and how are you accepting the "bait" and stepping into the trap?

Find a way to be more proactive, even in a situation you don't control.

●

As usual, time with Alena left Zoe feeling energized and in control. Instead of calling Alison, she decided to drop by the agency and say hello. On the way, she stopped by the florist and purchased a gift for Alison and the team.

"I don't have an appointment," Zoe explained to the receptionist. "Is Alison available?"

While the young man checked, Zoe mentally rehearsed her pitch. Oddly, she wasn't nervous at all. She was excited and eager to share her ideas with Alison.

"Alison has a conference call in ten minutes, but she'd love to say hi and set up an appointment with you when she has more time. She'll be right out to greet you."

Suddenly Zoe felt ridiculous standing there without an appointment, holding a bonsai tree meant to represent disciplined, deliberate growth. What had she been thinking! She needed to make a graceful exit.

"Oh, that's all right. I can come another time. I don't want to disturb Alison. I'll call her and set up an appointment."

It was too late. Alison appeared as promised. She greeted Zoe with an extended hand and a warm smile, "Zoe, thank you for stopping by. I was hoping to hear from you today. I wish I had more time to speak with you just now. Can we schedule a time to talk?"

Zoe was amazed at how such an extremely busy woman could make someone feel so welcome. Even without an appointment, she felt like an honored guest.

"Absolutely," she answered, juggling the bonsai awkwardly to shake Alison's hand. "I enjoyed meeting with the team and learning more about the new account. I do have some ideas I'd like to share with you.

For now, I'd like to leave you with a hint." Zoe presented the bonsai. "I can explain later when you have more time; it's a metaphor."

Alison laughed. "I can't wait!"

They set a time to meet the following day, and Zoe said good-bye. She was glad she had come, and she left thinking bonsai trees aren't ridiculous at all.

Actually, it had worked out perfectly. She had more time to organize her thoughts before meeting with Alison. That evening Zoe was back at the kitchen table surrounded by storyboards, Mind Maps, and a guide for bonsai enthusiasts. Her ideas were taking shape, and she was enjoying the process so much.

Madeline called twice, and Zoe ignored the incessant ringing. She wasn't ready to explain herself, and she knew Maddy would instantly know something was up. Zoe wasn't good at hiding things from Madeline.

The cat sauntered in nonchalantly, pretending not to care about the interesting work going on. After a few minutes, curiosity got the best of her, and Minnie jumped on the table to have a look. Normally Zoe would have shooed her off the table, but tonight she welcomed the company.

five

BOLD MOVES

Stealing Home

The morning air was cold, but the sun was shining brightly as Zoe set out. She arrived at the appointed time and was ushered almost immediately to Alison's office.

After greeting her warmly, Alison poured each of them a cup of coffee and sat in a chair across from Zoe. "The team has decided to accept the challenge, and I am very pleased with the plan." She gestured to a notebook sitting on the table between them. Next to that was the bonsai tree. "They've done an outstanding job."

Zoe smiled. "They are exceptional people, and this is an exciting opportunity."

"It is," Alison agreed. "But it is not without risk. We will need to manage our growth and resources very carefully. If you accepted a temporary assignment here, what role do you see yourself playing?" Alison was getting right to the point, but there was nothing abrupt in her tone. She was leaning forward with genuine interest.

The time had come.

"When I met with the team, I could see the plan coming together. I'd like to work with this team and with you very much." Zoe looked at the bonsai tree. "Some people think bonsai trees are just miniature versions of larger trees, and something cruel has been done to keep them small. I used to think that too, but it isn't true. Bonsais are a wonderful example of disciplined, deliberate growth. I think that's a good metaphor for what is happening here—growth that is elegant and purposeful. It takes understanding and commitment to grow a bonsai. There is a science to it, but it is also an art form." Zoe paused. Alison was listening intently.

"I left the team meeting with the sense I'd missed something important. I think I've discovered it now. Perhaps my role has nothing to do with the new account after all. Maybe I can be a resource to this team and to you by focusing on the accounts you already have—by supporting the account managers to protect what they have established."

Alison sat back in her chair, and Zoe wasn't sure what that meant. It was too late to back out now, so she forged ahead. Taking a cue from Alena, she used a question rather than an answer, "As the team works to accommodate the new account, what will that mean to your current clients?"

"That's a good question," Alison admitted. "I'd like to think our existing clients won't notice a difference at all."

"But as you grow into this opportunity and resources are stretched, it's likely they will notice a difference,"

Zoe countered. "A great deal of time and thought has gone into handling the new account. The missing piece may be a comprehensive plan for your existing clients. I'd like to be that resource—the person on your team who makes very sure nothing falls through the cracks. I can help you minimize the risk by maintaining and growing your base."

Alison was watching her intently, but she didn't say a word. Zoe pressed on.

"The first time I met you, you told the story of the bright red bag. It resonated with me because you were willing to share something you had learned—a personal insight. Then, at the team meeting you put that red bag on the table. You were applying the lesson in real time!

"I've learned something recently too. It is very possible to focus on the opportunity you are reaching for and lose sight of the one in your hand. I've learned how to grow and shape the opportunity that is present. I'd like to help you extend your reach by holding closely what you already have."

Alison was genuinely intrigued now. "Exactly how would you go about doing that?"

For the next twenty minutes Zoe shared her outline for client communication and care. She used the bonsai metaphor to demonstrate the art of training growth and shaping client expectations. When she had finished, she boldly added, "I understand this is a temporary support position to begin with. My personal plan is to become so valuable that you cannot imagine going on without me."

Zoe sat back in her chair and met Alison's eyes. There. She had done it, and regardless of the outcome, she felt wonderful inside. All of the work had come together—the three answers, her storyboard, and the Mind Maps had made it possible for her to tell this story very well.

"You've put your red bag on the table too," Alison said. She was smiling. "I love your story and how you've connected what you have learned with the very real challenge we are facing. You've invested yourself in this, Zoe, at a very personal level. That is true about the bonsai too—it takes a great deal of personal commitment and care. I appreciate the work you've done. Do you think one hundred days will give you enough time to become indispensable?"

Zoe was thrilled! "Yes!" she answered. "That is enough time for me to demonstrate value. I'm curious though; why one hundred days?"

WHAT IF YOU HAD ONE HUNDRED DAYS TO WRITE A SUCCESS STORY?

Every new job, assignment, or project brings with it the opportunity to create "faster wins." Presidents, CEOs, and even marathon runners use one hundred days as a benchmark for success. Transplant patients mark one hundred days as an important milestone, and students count the day as a turning point.

Some one-hundred-day plans are a flurry of activity without demonstrating measurable results. This is also known as "all the talk without the walk." It is mistaking activity for progress. (If I can just look busy, I might also look successful.)

Other plans are too aggressive—they try to attack too many things too quickly without a strategy or buy-in from the people who are impacted. And it's entirely possible to deliver results that aren't highly prized. The trick is to zero in on things that really matter and create momentum with authentic buy-in and commitment from others.

There is absolutely nothing stopping you from starting your own one-hundred-day clock right now! You don't need a new position or project to apply these principles. You can find a way to win faster and make those wins more obvious—right now, right where you are. Here are the steps you can take to implement an effective one-hundred-day plan of your own (and avoid the common pitfalls):

1. Assess the situation. Learn as much as you can about the goals and priorities of your organization. What is your organization trying to accomplish? What are the priorities of your department, team, and boss?

2. Find a tough problem to solve or capture an opportunity. What's working well and what isn't? Investigate!

3. Identify the people who can help you succeed. Seek advice and expertise. Gather perspectives.

4. Leverage your resources. Think about what you will need to be successful. Consider time, money, information, and even people.

5. Get others involved so they can be committed. Involvement invites ownership, and ownership inspires commitment.

6. Make progress visible and results obvious—create wins and winners.

Regardless of where you work or the role you play, these steps are available to you. Think about how you would put them into practice right where you are. Here's a story that demonstrates the steps beautifully.

Linda leads a team of cashiers for a large retail store in the Pacific Northwest. When she looked for a problem to solve, she found a tremendous opportunity—there was a huge problem in attendance and tardiness. She worked with her manager and human resources to calculate the size of the problem and its impact on the bottom line. (Those figures were staggering, and that got everyone's attention! Now Linda knew she was working on something of extreme value.)

After thoroughly researching the issue, Linda devised a targeted one-hundred-day plan to reduce occurrences by 60 percent. She was able to put a dollar figure next to that percentage; the number was impressive. With a goal in place, Linda identified the people who could help her succeed.

An associate from the finance department helped her build a model for tracking occurrences. This allowed her to generate a weekly report, making progress more visible and results more obvious.

She leveraged her resources by engaging cashiers in the solution. Her team developed contests, participated in building the schedule, and found creative ways to recognize outstanding attendance.

One of the most compelling aspects of this story is how Linda connected people with the strategy. Cashiers who had typically felt very "low" on the value chain of the organization were now co-creators of a brilliant cost-saving initiative. Their efforts were visible and valuable.

Because Linda had demonstrated how her plan would save money and improve customer service, she was able to negotiate for some exciting incentives. Morale soared, attendance improved, and turnover went down.

Her plan was more than successful. Linda solved a tough

problem and created a big win with many winners. She found ways to leverage her resources of time, information, money, and even people. She involved the right people and made progress very visible.

Through this process you will grow! "What a learning experience!" Linda remembers. "I worked with people across the organization to size and solve the problem. Those relationships are extremely valuable to this day. Other teams have duplicated our plan, so the model continues to impact the bottom line. We've become the 'attendance-improvement experts' for the organization. We're very proud of the difference we made. It's a really fun story to tell!"

I encourage you to devise and implement your one-hundred-day plan. This isn't just a management exercise. These are the steps all of us can take to become indispensable, create a niche, build our brand, and deliver enduring value. (Even as I write this, I am starting the clock on another one-hundred-day plan of my own. This is very exciting stuff—like a 100-yard dash with a long-distance strategy. When you get to the end of the sprint, you may find you have changed the entire race.)

DEVELOP A NETWORKING STRATEGY THAT SUPPORTS AND PROMOTES YOUR PLAN

If you study successful people, you will find relationships are at the very core of their achievements. They don't pretend to have all the answers. They surround themselves with extraordinary people, and they have learned how to tell the story and how to get people on board. Networking is both a priority and a discipline. Executive recruiter and author Bob Beaudine offers this advice: "If you're going to fulfill your destiny in life, you're going to need some wise friends and advisors to help you see a vision of your future that perhaps you can't see yourself."[1]

It's interesting to note that when they find themselves in a career crisis, people are often more likely to contact strangers than to work their own network! "Out of shame or embarrassment, they don't call their friends. Rather they turn to faceless websites, hand out business cards to strangers, and send out letters that start out 'Dear Recruiter.'"[2]

Many women recognize they don't have the network they need to be more successful in their current or future positions. Even if they do appreciate the power of networking, they may not have a real strategy for building their personal and professional network. Often women admit they are trying to do it all on their own without the strength and support a network can provide.

Time is certainly a factor. The best networking I've seen is a strategic, intentional discipline. But how do we add these activities to a cup that's already full and sloshing over the sides? Perhaps we must first decide that networking is of real value and determine to make it a real priority.

In a worldwide poll of fifteen thousand senior executives, the online business networking service www.MeettheBoss.com reports that executives are spending an additional eleven hours each month online sharing their professional experiences and learning from their peers. "I find online business networking very useful," says MeettheBoss member Oliver Bruns, head of polyurethanes at Bayer Material Sciences. "It allows me to create or join a discussion and get immediate answers and experiences from like-minded professionals on issues such as regulation or technology."[3]

Networking is powerful, and technology has blown the doors off the time and space boundaries. Suddenly your colleagues are around the world, in every time zone, representing every industry! Technology has also leveled the playing field, and resources are available to you regardless of your position, title, or experience level. You can ask a question, join a discussion, or "virtually eavesdrop" on the experts as they problem solve and share experiences.

Networking online will not replace the face-to-face version, but most experts agree it's a valuable add to your networking strategy. Online social networking allows you to build your brand and your niche. As you forge relationships and share ideas with people across town and around the world, you can establish yourself as a "thought leader" in your field or discipline.

Have you ever considered yourself a potential "thought leader?" That is more than possible!

Project management is a good example of networking to learn from the masters. Before managing your first real project, you can tap into the "knowledge shelf," learn about certifications and credentials, and connect with a local chapter of the Project Management Institute (www.pmi.org). And that's just one example of the resources available to you!

Would you like to carve out a niche or brand yourself as an expert? Whether it's blogging for profit, public speaking, mentoring, negotiating, or customer service, there is a network of people who are developing the skills, answering the questions, and building the relationships. You can join them! Right where you are is the perfect launching place.

The most effective networking occurs in the context of your map or plan. Because the possibilities are limitless, you will want to focus on the area of keen interest. With your long-term goals and brand in mind, take a moment to answer these questions:

1. What skills or disciplines do I want to learn more about?

2. Where do I want to develop expertise?

3. What is the niche I want to create for myself?

4. What do I want to be known for?

Questions like these will help you frame your networking efforts and put them into context. The next step is to evaluate your existing network. Grab a piece of paper and create three columns as shown below.

A	B	C

There are the people you know and who know you. You can call on each other and be resources for each other. The communication is natural and frequent. You might call this your "A" list or inner circle.

Next, think of the people who skirt the "A" list. You know of them, and they may know of you. Until now, you haven't interacted with them often; they are more like acquaintances. This is your "B" list.

Finally, with your goals in mind, whom do you want to meet? I encourage you to imagine networking with the most successful and influential people in your fields of interest. Work from your map to think of people who are known for the skills you want to develop and the brand you want to build. These are your "Cs."

You aren't finished with your lists just yet. Review them with questions like these in mind:

1. What have the people on your "A" list done for you?

2. How have these people been a resource to you?

3. What have you done to let them know of their role in your successes?

4. What have you done for your "A" list lately?

5. What are they trying to accomplish?

6. How can you help them succeed?

7. What can you do to become a more valuable resource to your "A" list?

8. Whom do you know that might be a valuable contact for the people on your "A" list?

9. Looking at your "B" list, whom would you like to know better?

10. What is your plan to move these people from the "B" list to the "A" list?

11. Who are the experts in your field of interest?

12. How do you plan to meet them?

Evaluating the network you have and setting specific goals for the network you want to build is a powerful strategy. I hope you will take the time to craft it. Next are some high-impact tips that will help you hit the ground running.

NETWORKING TOP TEN (OK, ELEVEN)

1. Develop a networking strategy. Decide what you are trying to accomplish through networking. Your "why" is important. It shapes the "who" and "where."

2. Become an authority and a thought leader. Make presentations, write articles, blog, and become more visibly active in trade associations.

3. Leverage technology. Make sure your online presence makes a positive impression.

4. Put the "Law of Reciprocity" to work. Focus on what you can give. Find ways to make yourself increasingly valuable and essential to your network.

5. "Touch" your network frequently. Set an appointment with yourself each week, even for twenty minutes, to pick up the phone, jot a personal note, or make an introduction.

6. Upgrade your image. Make sure the personal impression you make is consistent with the brand you want to build.

7. Remember, the fast track to believability is likeability.[4] Listen more than you talk. Engage others with questions.

8. Build a knowledge base, not a database. Names, addresses, and phone numbers are part of a database. A knowledge base is much, much more than that. It would include understanding the goals, concerns, and needs of your contacts. A knowledge base points to a relationship, not a Rolodex.

9. Build it before you need it, and build it in. Make it your best practice to meet people and make the connections. Meetings, social events, and even waiting in line can be prime opportunities to build your network. Take the social initiative. Throw your hand out, ask questions, and get people talking about their favorite subject—themselves!

10. Look at who's on the list and who should be. Set goals for your network. Whom do you want to add? How can you make that happen? Look at your current network too. How can you help them, and how can they help you?

11. Look for information that adds value. I learned this one from a brilliant networker, Harvey Mackay. If you know the interests and goals of the people in your knowledge base, you can look for information and news relevant to them.

DIAL IT UP A NOTCH AND CREATE MORE SYNERGY WITH MASTERMIND GROUPS

The concept of mastermind groups was originally conceived by Napoleon Hill. Hill commissioned Andrew Carnegie to locate the formula for success. Over twenty years, Carnegie studied five hundred of the most successful people of his time. The research was first presented in the course titled "The Law of Success"[5] and ultimately became the much acclaimed *Think and Grow Rich* (also referred to as TAGR)[6] with more than thirty million copies sold.[7]

Masterminding is a marvelous example of peer coaching and mentoring where a group of people gather to focus on a problem, opportunity, skill, or discipline. Members contribute knowledge and experience or questions and needs around the mastermind topic. Synergy is created as members think with purpose toward personal or professional goals.

What does a mastermind group look like?

Typically, mastermind groups have three to six members. The group meets frequently and consistently to support the goals of the membership. This might be monthly, bimonthly, or even weekly. The meetings can be face-to-face or virtual, so the group is not constricted by geography.

Professions need not limit the group either. Some of the most powerful experiences come from groups with varied backgrounds and fields of interest. It is fantastic what you can learn from people who work in different industries. Masterminding invites eclectic perspective!

The agenda may be fluid, according to the needs of the members, but it is purpose-filled. Members update each other on current states, debrief action items, and raise issues for discussion.

Mastermind groups solve problems, practice skills, and mark progress. The key is that members come with a challenge or an obstacle they cannot see their way around. They offer it to the group for assistance in developing a strategy. The entire group benefits from the process of exploring the issue and solving the problem.

The group can work on more than one problem at a time, and they often do. The process is important. Groups must establish ground rules and operating agreements. These simply answer the question, "How will we do business with each other?"

Accountability is a major theme of mastermind groups (MMG). Members hold themselves and each other accountable for the contributions they make—what they bring to and take from the group. Both sides of that equation are essential to the ecosystem of an MMG. Without this kind of giving and receiving, energy will drain from the group, and it will eventually implode.

As relationships forge and trust is established, support for personal and professional goals may spill over the framework of scheduled meetings. Members may reach out to give or ask for additional support.

Mastermind groups have been around for a long time, and they've been called lots of things. A global organization headquartered in Houston, Texas, calls them talent teams and is quite intentional about launching them.

I had the wonderful opportunity to work with one of these teams. What a pleasure it was to meet with this handpicked group of men and women called to solve a persistent problem: retaining and promoting talented women in a male-dominated industry.[8]

This talent team represents an authentic commitment to find, keep, and grow women in the engineering industry. It also recognizes challenges women face in the workplace and in their other life roles. To answer the question and solve the problem, this organization formed the team, created the focus, and looks forward to the recommendations.

As the group came together from around the country, they focused first on the process. Here are the first steps they took:

1. Defining purpose: What exactly are we here to accomplish?

2. Establishing ground rules: How will we work together?

3. Clarifying roles and responsibilities: How will each of us make a valuable contribution?

4. Determining structure and process: How will we structure ourselves, and what processes will we use to get real traction?

5. Ensuring accountability: How will we measure success?

In just a few hours, the group created a problem statement, drafted operating agreements, and brainstormed action items. The larger team broke into smaller groups, each focusing on a specific element of the issue. It was interesting to see people volunteer for parts of the project that would normally fall outside of their daily disciplines and skill set. For example, the person in charge of financial analysis offered to consult on that piece, but she intentionally joined the group charged with developing an organizational survey. She offered her skills as a resource and created a growth opportunity for herself.

Masterminding can also be applied at a very personal and spiritual level. Retreats are a great example. By definition, a retreat is a "place of peace" or refuge. Here you might see coaching, mentoring, and networking blended with the concept of masterminding. In a retreat setting, participants confront themselves to the core, locate vision and purpose, and confront barriers.

Tammy, a certified coach, and Krista, a retreat participant, shared this story about a Living Your Vision course in the Pacific Northwest.[9]

"The process is part masterminding and part guided facilitation," Tammy explained. "The retreat process is designed to take people away so they can focus on gaining clarity around their values, vision, and purpose. The guided facilitation takes place over three days. This process can be done in groups or one-on-one. I have found that the power is again in the group process just like with masterminding—there is power in numbers.

"Prior to the retreat, there is significant work to be done by the participants. They assess where their satisfaction is with their current life. Taking a picture of 'where I am now' and 'what I value the most' is essential in developing the plan of 'where I want to go next.'

"During the retreat, the group develops a close bond. They hold each other accountable for discovering what is most important. In one of my favorite elements, each member shares stories they have prepared ahead of time. As the stories are told, other members capture words that get to the heart or essence of the individual speaking.

"A key component of the process is when individuals identify their core essence to define their vision and purpose. It's an inside-out model. We have to understand what's going on inside to create a plan for what we want on the outside.

"After the retreat, the group embarks upon a twelve-week group coaching session. This is done by telephone or in person, depending on the structure and location of the group. The coaching process is run like a mastermind in that members have such a close bond that they can very effectively and powerfully challenge assumptions and question anyone who is 'under-living' based on their goals. The group coaching is where people really get into life mapping—setting intentions for the key areas of life and putting in place the choices and actions that support their intentions."

"For me, the retreat was the intense part," Krista shared. "The emotional discovery, vision exercises, and self-connection were uncomfortable at times. When we began on the first day, I realized this type of introspective: seeking God 'work' is difficult. People in general do not take the time, nor do they usually have a clear process, to do so. This work is absolutely essential. God gives us pieces and glimpses of His future plans for us. He does not give us the full picture with an outline of all the steps necessary to get there. The process of discovery can be challenging, yet very necessary and ultimately satisfying work."

As Tammy and Krista told me about their experiences, I was reminded of how powerful our stories are. They hold important keys for unlocking possibility!

If you were to share three stories about yourself, what would they be? I encourage you to write them down and find a way to share them. Listen to them too. What themes are woven through? What do your stories say about who you are and what matters most?

This truly is inside-out work and a great example of masterminding and coaching. As we make ourselves available for this kind of exploration and surround ourselves with people who are equally invested in the process, we break through!

As you can see, masterminding is not just for the professional you. Consider this strategy for your personal, physical, financial, and spiritual goals as well. In *Ready, Set... Grow!* I presented the balance wheel exercise for life. As you grow professionally, you absolutely must build your life on a solid foundation. It's quite possible to be wildly successful in your job while your life falls apart.[10]

With these examples in mind, you may be participating in a form of masterminding without even realizing it. If so, perhaps you can use this information to increase the effectiveness of your group by viewing it as masterminding and applying more of those disciplines. If you aren't plugged into a group, I hope you will look into this strategy. It's brilliant, really, allowing you time to give and receive energy, ideas, and encouragement. This kind of soul searching might also reveal a bold new move.

WHAT DO BOLD MOVES LOOK LIKE?

On July 3, 2009, Sarah Palin surprised the country with a decision to step down eighteen months before her term ended as governor of Alaska. She made the announcement in what appeared to be an impromptu speech. It seemed to be so quickly arranged (or a secret so carefully guarded) that even the press had a hard time getting there to cover it!

Her announcement created quite the media buzz. A firestorm of opinions quickly ensued about what it meant. Comments ranged from "brilliant" to "irresponsible" and everything in between. Speculation swirled as bloggers, journalists, and political commentators analyzed her intentions. The country waited for another shoe to drop.

Was she just avoiding political scandal? Were indictments eminent? Why was she really stepping down? Is a megamillion-dollar-book deal a good trade for future political positions, or is this bold move her way of rewriting the rules?

I listened and watched as news commentators debated it. Many political analysts predicted her decision would harm any future political aspirations she might have. Even with a strong base of followers, abandoning her post does not look good on a hopeful president's résumé, they explained. Others applauded her for "going rogue" (which is also the title of her new book).

As I watched all of this unfold, one thing became very clear to me. Sarah Palin broke the rules. She made a bold move.

My purpose here isn't to analyze Palin's strategy or critique her motives. I want to talk about women who make bold moves and, whether we agree with them or not, what we can learn from them. Here is my short list. What would you add?

- It's possible to advance in a different direction. Stepping down doesn't necessarily mean stepping back. "She's not retreating, she's reloading" became a slogan on Palin's book tour.[11]

- Your brand is the platform you build. From there you can reinvent yourself in surprising ways.

- Your message becomes the brand, and the brand becomes the message. Unconventional may be an understatement when it comes to Palin, and that's exactly what she's going for.

- Bold moves and big platforms make great targets. Make sure you are grounded by your values and a compelling vision.

- Bold moves will cost you something. (Price tags might include things like approval, popularity, comfort, or even cash.)

- Bold moves can also pay off in a big way. Before it was released, Palin's book set some impressive sales records.

- If you realize that you can't achieve your goals from where you are, a bold move may be required. (And you can be very sure not everyone will agree with your decision! People who share your values may have something to say, and you can bet those who don't will!)

- Have your speaking points ready, be consistent, and don't underestimate the power of social media to get your message through.

- There's something else here—a subtle move. Palin didn't chase the news; she became news. (That actually could be brilliant.)

- Lots of people will have advice for you. Make sure you surround yourself with wise counsel and people who will help you stay grounded and centered.

- Be strategic. Make sure your current move won't limit future moves. Don't box yourself in with a shortsighted move.

- You may be *invited* to defend your moves. RSVP with care. Your moves should reflect and protect what you value most. Even when they do, your motives may be challenged.

- Bold moves that don't add real value will look more like an ego out of control. Platforms built to promote self are shaky and temporary. That means your message must resonate.

- Accept (or don't accept) the fact that the rules are different for men and women on the playing field. There are dozens of examples, but let me toss just one out there. When a man in the political arena says to the media, "Keep your hands off my family," it's noble and respectable. When a woman says virtually the same thing, it's called weak and whiny. Women immediately hear things like, "If you can't stand the heat" (I cannot even bear to finish that old, tired cliché. Here I am inserting my own heavy sigh.)

I encourage you to step away from the political aspects of Palin's story and use it to think about your own bold moves!

1. What risks should you be taking?

2. What do you need to let go of in order to accomplish your goals?

3. What keeps you from taking the next step and making a move?

4. Does the need for everyone's stamp of approval keep you from making a bold move?

5. Where do your work and values collide (and what are you going to do about that)?

6. What is your platform? How does that base elevate you so you can see further and accomplish more?

What will your bold move look like? There are plenty of bold moves in the headlines. Here are a few I've seen recently on the front lines—just everyday people doing extraordinary things:

- Carla works in the restaurant of a hotel but dreams of writing. In her words, she cannot imagine being anything but a writer. She is the youngest member of a writing club and boldly shares her work for others to review and critique. She is freelancing now, and a few of her stories have been published. Writing has become more than a dream. (She may be serving soup on the side, but she is an author!)

- When I met Natalie, she was an engineer in Birmingham. She left a lucrative job in the telecommunications industry to follow her calling—working with youth to "provoke self-sufficiency." Natalie has developed seven empowering programs addressing motivation, education, entrepreneurship, and home ownership. (I love hearing from Natalie. Attached to her last e-mail was a copy of a grant letter she has worked so hard to secure. She is on her way!)

- Susan is a customer service representative in a call center. After celebrating her forty-sixth birthday, she went back to school to get her nursing degree. Her bold move reminds us it is never too late to begin!

My own bold move was leaving corporate America and a banking career to become a consultant (that might be considered code for "unemployed"). I was the classic example of generalized discontent. I had achieved many of my professional goals, but I wasn't in love with my work. When I resigned to pursue a speaking and consulting career, a gentleman colleague said (with a shake of his head, a cluck of his tongue, and deep concern in his tone), "That's a really big leap."

Yes, it was. It was a really big, heart-clutching, hold-on-to-your-hat leap. I have just one word for him now: "TADA!"

Make no mistake; it was hard work, and there were sacrifices. There were also setbacks and disappointments. I think of those sacrifices and setbacks as investments now, and they have paid off beautifully. As I write this book, I have another bold move in mind. (You'll have to stay tuned for that one.)

Your bold move may not involve a change in career or company. It might be presenting an idea, taking a stand, improving a process, or stepping up to a new challenge.

Incidentally, bold moves require research! These are not impulsive, fly-by-the-seat-of-your-pants whims. They are strategic plans executed with precision. Moves like these push hard on the four elements of your high-performance zone. They challenge you to manage perspective, leadership, capabilities, and resources in new ways.

GET YOUR MOVE ON!

This week, be on the lookout for bold moves. Study the moves and the people who make them. You may find these in the headlines or on the job. While you're at it, think about what your own bold move might look like.

You might even try a form of masterminding the medical profession has been practicing (in one form or another) since the seventeenth century. It's called grand rounds.

On television, rounds are a dramatic test. Residents walk briskly down the hospital corridor following a very serious doctor. The entire group piles into a patient's room, and one of the residents nervously steps forward. Aware that all eyes are upon her, she introduces the case: "This is my patient Mrs. Jones. She arrived yesterday presenting these symptoms."

Treatments are discussed, assumptions are challenged, and a plan of action is created. This is learning in real time with live patients!

What if you were the business case? Step back for a moment and imagine a group of business "doctors" discussing your situation. What symptoms are you "presenting"? What is the diagnosis? What plan of action would they devise? What protocols would they recommend?

I encourage you to do two things. Find your professional advisory board and present your case.

———————————————————●———————————————————

Driving home from her meeting with Alison, Zoe had another serious meeting with her windshield. "Alison expects personal leadership from all of her team members. I think I understand the big picture and the overall strategy, but I need an action plan that will get real traction. I want to create a fast win. I need to write a success story with this opportunity. I have a lot to learn, and the clock is already ticking."

Suddenly, Zoe was overwhelmed with panic. She had been sure of herself as she had presented the outline to Alison. Now she felt her confidence ebbing away. "This is a giant test, and I don't know the answers," she pleaded with the windshield. "I'm not even sure about the questions. How do you study for an exam like that?"

As usual, the windshield had nothing to offer. She gave it a dirty look and drove on in perplexed silence.

Just ahead was a city park. This was one of Zoe's favorite walking and thinking places. She parked the car and pulled on her coat. Perhaps the fresh air would inspire her.

Along the path she stopped to watch a group of people who looked at first like an acrobat troop. They were running, jumping, and flipping over rails and walls. It was amazing to watch, especially when she realized they were actually using the obstacles in their path to move through the air! What most people would walk around, they were launching from. The movements were graceful, and they made it look effortless. It was fantastic!

"Have you heard of *parkour*?" one of the athletes asked her.

Zoe told him she had not, and he went on to explain. "This is very big in Europe, and it is catching on here. *Parkour* is a physical discipline. The goal is to get from one point to another as efficiently as possible, using your body and the environment. You overcome obstacles like rocks, branches—even architecture—by interacting with them."

"It looks very difficult and a little dangerous," thought Zoe aloud.

The young man laughed, "It's great training both physically and mentally. The movements of *parkour* are natural. As you learn to move, you build strength, balance, and endurance. You learn to trust yourself too. It's not just a physical activity; it's about problem solving, clarity, and confidence. You become very aware of your surroundings. A male practitioner is called a *traceur*, and a female is called a *traceuse*. Our local club is really growing. Would you like to try it sometime?"

Zoe smiled. "I think I will try it—at work."

"I want to think and move like a *traceuse*," Zoe decided to herself as she walked on. "I want to overcome obstacles with speed and grace. I want to be more aware of my surroundings, solve problems efficiently, and learn how to trust myself more."

The walk had been a very good idea. Even though she didn't have all the answers, she felt surprising calm. "The answers will come," she reassured herself. "The answers will come because I am asking for them and I am watching for them. My answers are on the way."

A light mist began to fall, and Zoe turned on the windshield wipers. With each swipe of the blades, she could see the road more clearly in front of her.

six

SELF-DEFINING MOVES

Setting Yourself Apart

Once home, Zoe made a quick call to Alena. She was excited to share the good news about what she was now calling the one-hundred-day audition.

"It feels like an audition," she explained to Alena. "I have one hundred days to demonstrate value and earn a place on this team." Even as she said it, Zoe felt her stomach tighten.

Alena was enthusiastic and supportive. "This is very exciting, Zoe. I cannot wait to see how this opportunity unfolds. I have no doubt that you will audition well for this role and win an even bigger part!"

"Thank you, Alena. I'm thrilled to have this opportunity, and I appreciate your confidence." Zoe shared Alena's enthusiasm, but she was having a little trouble with the doubt-free part. *Parkour* disciplines were flying around in her head as she tried to recapture the resolve she'd felt earlier in the park.

Alena seemed to sense her anxiety. "Are you free tonight? My husband has a board meeting, and I have an idea. It may be just what you need to get into character and study for your new role."

"I am free." Zoe smiled at how easily Alena picked up and ran with the audition metaphor. "What do you have in mind?"

"Let's call it a big surprise," Alena said dramatically. "I'll pick you up at seven thirty. Wear comfortable clothes, something you can move in easily."

Zoe laughed. "Uh oh, what am I getting myself into here?" Alena wasn't telling, and Zoe was both intrigued and anxious. Mostly she was thankful for the distraction. She felt it was time to step away from the intensity of these past few days and let her mind rest.

Alena arrived in comfortable clothes, and Zoe thought, "How does this woman manage to look elegant and casual at the same time?" She had come to admire Alena so much and was constantly amazed at Alena's capacity to give. What a wonderful mentor and friend.

Her thoughts were interrupted when Alena said, "This is going to be fantastic, Zoe! It is something I've wanted to do for a long time. When you told me about your one-hundred-day audition, it sparked the idea."

As they drove, Zoe shared what she had learned about *parkour*. "How interesting," Alena said. "I can't see myself flipping over a stone ledge or running up a wall, but it is a great picture of overcoming barriers and solving problems."

A moment later they parked in front of the Community Centre for Performing Arts. Zoe asked, "Are we going to a play?"

Alena nodded. "Actually, we are going to be in the play. We're attending an improvisation workshop!"

Zoe froze in her seat. This was not good. She managed to push words of protest out of her mouth. "Oh, Alena, I don't know. Maybe I can just watch. I am not very comfortable getting up in front of people." That sounded so much better than the conversation happening in her head: "I will throw up if I have to do this. Honestly, I will." Unconsciously she squeezed her fingers tightly together. This is not the time for complete disclosure!

Alena reassured her, "Zoe, this is not a test. I want you to relax and enjoy yourself. Whether you observe or act, improv is a marvelous learning tool. You love metaphors. I think you will find this one is quite profound."

WORK IS AN IMPROV THEATER (AND YES, YOU CAN ACT)

A favorite presentation of mine is titled, "Thinking on Your Feet: Improvising at Work!" People love this workshop and the principles it teaches. Improvisation really is a wonderful jolt! It builds confidence, communication, and presentation skills by asking us to respond creatively and spontaneously. It strengthens our ability to solve problems and work through difficult situations.

Improv makes us laugh too. It reminds us to use our imagination more, to play and find humor in unexpected places.

The art of improv is not the art of having perfect words and clever answers on the tip of your tongue. It's learning to trust yourself, expand your comfort zone, and reach for more imaginative approaches. Improv is learning how to take what is offered and running with it to move the scene forward.

Authors Mark Bergen, Molly Cox, and Jim Detmar give us this definition of improvisation: "Improvisation is a process—the process in which something new and exciting is created in a moment of spontaneity—a flash of discovery ignited by a spark of imagination."[1]

Improvisation is based on accepting or embracing offers to advance the scene. The scene might be an impatient doctor delivering news to a patient, with one twist: players must begin each sentence with the next unused letter in the alphabet. The doctor starts with sentences beginning with A, the patient responds with statements that start with B, and so on—all the way through the alphabet.

This is not an easy game to play! Each response is an offer—like a game of tennis, back and forth across the net, giving and receiving, working with and adding to what has been offered, each side sharing control of the story line.

Life and work are built on responding to offers as well. Our "scenes" may include a:

- Difficult co-worker who snaps at you in front of others

- Boss who communicates poorly

- Member of your team who fails to complete assignments

- Family member who criticizes you

- Friend who is asking for advice

- Deadline that is daunting

- Goal that takes your breath away

- Problem blocking your path

We all have the opportunity to improvise! Life is brimming with offers. They invite a response, and the scenes move forward. We don't always control what is offered, but we can advance with an objective. In many ways, we can influence and direct how the scene plays out.

Before reading on, how would you answer the following question: How is life (and work) like practicing the art of improvisation?

As I think about that question and review Improv Comedy's glossary of improvisational terms,[2] here's what comes to mind:

- Life cannot be memorized. There is no script.

- We are always on stage. We are always presenting, even to an audience of one.

- We fall into patterns of behavior (and some of them aren't successful).

- Life is spontaneous. Somehow we must respond!

- We accept offers to advance the scene. (It's considered "wimping" to accept an offer without acting on it.)

- Blocking or rejecting ideas from other players is a common problem for new improvisers. (This can be a common workplace problem too, and not just for "new" people.)

- We work in context. Individual scenes play out in a broader setting.

- Life and work are filled with conflict. (If there is no conflict, the scene may be dull.)

- We must overcome obstacles and solve problems to achieve our objectives.
- We don't always know the objectives of the other performers.
- We must keep our objectives firmly in mind.
- If we trust ourselves, we are more effective.
- Life is supposed to be fun! It's OK to play!
- We really have to pay attention and be present to the moment.
- Listening is important, and most of us don't do it very well. (We are too busy thinking ahead to formulate our own responses.)
- Life is a collaborative effort. We must build on the ideas of others.
- Focus is important. Experienced improvisers know how to smoothly share the focus and control of a scene.
- There is an opportunity to explore and heighten ideas. We can follow ideas to see where they go and raise the stakes!
- There are different styles and approaches.
- We have to incorporate the unexpected.
- If a scene is overloaded with too much information, it's difficult to resolve the conflict or reach a satisfying conclusion.

- If we take over the scene and don't allow other players to influence the outcome, we aren't very popular!

- And this may be my personal favorite from the improv lexicon: Charm is the quality that causes an audience to enjoy watching an actor.

No wonder successful business people are using theater arts to hone their skills and improve results! As I review that list, the business implications are incredible.

Studying the art of improvisation, I've picked up the basic rules. These guidelines can help us maneuver our own tough scenarios and difficult "scenes." For example, one premise of improvisation is: *You may change your approach, but you must keep your eye on the objective.* That's excellent advice! Remain focused on the goal and flexible in your approach.

Think about your own offers for a moment. What are the challenging scenarios you face right now at work? Reframe these as "offers," and think about how you will respond. How would the rules of improvisation change the way your difficult scene plays out?

- Have an objective.

- Keep your objective in mind at all times.

- Everything you say or do must be directed toward accomplishing your goal.

- Focus on the other actors.

- Be aware of the audience; sometimes they become part of the play.

- Accept the "offers." Work with what you are given.

- Keep trying to reach your objective until you are instructed to stop.

- Respond naturally to the situation. Try not to stereotype or play a "role."

If you decide to explore the possibilities of improvisation, here are seven things you can do right now to take the stage, sharpen your senses, and move your scenes forward:

1. Set a goal to try something new every week. Intentionally break your patterns and make room for innovation—even eccentricity!

2. Learn how to tell your stories well. People respond to and remember stories long after data escapes them.

3. Catch yourself blocking and rejecting offers. Instead of resisting what is offered, practice building on the ideas of others by saying, "Yes, and..."

4. Be very present to the moment.

5. Look for what you haven't seen before.

6. Listen for what you haven't heard.

7. Give yourself permission to play!

As you can see, there are dozens of benefits to improvisation. As you call on your personal resourcefulness, you may find a more confident, innovative person emerging. (She's in there somewhere, I promise!) You may learn to trust yourself more, take risks, share control, and speak up. You might even remember how to play. Your self-awareness will increase as you tune in to the responses and reactions of others. I'm certain you'll learn how to give and receive, and that is more powerful than you might imagine.

In their book *The Go-Giver*, authors Bob Burg and John David Mann offer Five Laws of Stratospheric Success.[3] The fifth law (my personal favorite) is the law of receptivity. This one resonates with me.

Are you open to giving and receiving?

Before reading *The Go-Giver*, if you had asked me that question, my answer would have been, "Well, of course." (I would have had resisted every temptation to roll my eyes just a bit, thinking what a silly question that is.)

Then I took a little test illustrated in the book. I invite you to try it right now. Take a deep breath. Gather as much oxygen into your lungs as you can—then slowly exhale while counting to thirty. Continue to push the air out of your lungs until you reach that goal!

If you are like most people, you became totally deflated somewhere around twelve.

This demonstration makes an important point: we must inhale *and* exhale. "Receiving is the natural result of giving," say Burg and Mann.[4] Some people are very good at inhaling (receiving), and others are comfortable with exhaling (giving). Successful people have learned to do both! They breathe! They breathe, and they make it look natural like…breathing.

Here's the part of that little "law" that really landed in my heart: If you are not open to receiving, you are blocking the flow! Successful people look for opportunities to give, and they are also comfortable receiving wisdom, comfort, counsel, and so on.

I had to really work on that. I am much more comfortable giving. It's sometimes hard for me to receive. Low receptivity means we might not ask for or accept help. Perhaps we think we should be able to do it all. Or maybe we think we should have all the answers, and it's hard to ask the questions. Receiving might make us feel vulnerable. I had to admit that my pride sometimes keeps me from receiving. Can you relate to that? (By the way, *The Go-Giver* is a must-read in my book. The story is marvelous, the laws are insightful, the authors are inspiring, and I am learning how to breathe better.)

When we learn to enter the flow of giving and receiving—accepting and responding to the offers presented—we will find ways to increase our value. As in *parkour*, our movements will be more natural. Challenges become resources as we use them to explore new approaches and break free of old patterns. Through this process we become more of a resource to others. That is the beautiful paradox: *when we learn how to receive, we have so much more to give.*

INCREASE YOUR VALUE BY PRODUCING REAL-TIME SOLUTIONS

Regardless of your position, you have the opportunity to do something extraordinary at work. *In great companies that is the expectation.* Chip Ray, an executive vice president for a global organization, shares a brilliant concept and a marvelous example.

Chip developed the Boulder Philosophy patterned after Dr. Stephen Covey's time management principle of putting first things first.[5] Covey demonstrates his formula for maximizing time resources by filling a glass jar with rocks first, then pebbles, followed by sand.

Rocks represent the highest priorities, pebbles illustrate tasks with less impact, and sand represents what is minor. This demonstration teaches us to focus on the important tasks (rocks) instead of being distracted and derailed by smaller issues (pebbles and sand). If we put sand and pebbles into the jar first, there won't be room for the rocks, which represent the real priorities.

The Boulder Philosophy gives every employee the opportunity to derive internal and external value by leading a major project or developing an idea. When complete, all boulders include a deliverable that people can see, touch, or hear—a rollout or communication plan and a way of measuring value.

In all cases, employees help define the project and, in turn, the desired outcome based on their own initiative and interests. Typically the boulder project is outside (or slightly outside) the person's day-to-day area of responsibility. This adds a development component to the project and an opportunity for networking. Some boulders are big; others are relatively small. Some are quick; others take a long time.

From a management perspective, the key to success is defining a value-added project that a person can handle while stretching their capabilities and encouraging them to grow.

"Whenever a boulder is completed, the project leader is recognized by the team and senior management. We actually give out engraved rocks recognizing the person with the name of the boulder and the date it was accomplished," Chip explains.[6]

When your team or organization follows the Boulder Philosophy, the outcomes you will see are impressive:

- A steady stream of innovative and valuable projects pushed over the finish line

- Fulfilled, motivated, and developing employees across all levels of the organization

- Better teamwork and company-wide networking

- Management that is constantly thinking about and looking for ways to increase value

- Meaningful projects, aligned with the strategy of the organization

"If you want to move mountains, you need to push boulders," Chip says.[7] He shares this excellent example:

Lynn was an administrative assistant in the global marketing department of CB&I. She had been an administrative assistant for nearly fifteen years, and although she wouldn't admit it, she was frustrated that her talents weren't being fully utilized.

When brainstorming about her next boulder, she focused on safety, one of the company's core values. Although it was unrelated to her day-to-day activities, it was something she was passionate about. She wanted to develop a tool that would help promote the importance of safety (at home, at work, and on the road). She also wanted to ensure that whatever she developed would be something people would use regularly to continually reinforce the safety message.

Lynn built on an idea she'd seen years earlier. She envisioned a deck of playing cards containing safety messages linked to the suits in the deck. (Hearts for safety at home—home is where the heart is. Spades for safety on the job site—using tools safely, and so on.)

Working with the company's safety group, she wrote a series of short safety messages and had a team develop accompanying graphics. Crafting fifty-two messages with appropriate images for a very culturally diverse group of employees at home and on job sites throughout the world was a real challenge. In addition, producing and distributing the cards at a reasonable price proved to be difficult.

In the end, Lynn overcame every challenge and sent out more than twenty-five thousand decks of cards for employees and customers on six continents! The feedback has been tremendous.

Since the first run, the cards have been translated into other languages, clients have asked for permission to reproduce the cards for their own use, and the company has used the cards to stimulate safety topics at the beginning of meetings.

Shortly after Lynn completed this boulder, she was promoted to a marketing specialist role within the company.

There are so many reasons to love this story!

Lynn found a way to blend her passion, skill, and creativity to create something of enduring value. (Incidentally, I have a deck of these cards. They are fabulous!) Lynn also involved others in this success. She invited others to be part of something special, which is another great example of creating a win and creating winners. Like a *traceuse*, Lynn cleared significant hurdles by interacting with the environment and leveraging the company's commitment to safety.

Perhaps you've been in that place of frustration, feeling that your talents and gifts were sidelined or invisible. Are you ready to increase your value by producing real-time solutions? I hope Lynn's story will inspire you to find your own "boulders" and make them move!

That said, you can push lots of rocks around the workplace without establishing a solid brand. In addition to managing the rocks, plan how you will manage the message! In the next chapter you'll learn how to present your value and forge your brand.

GET YOUR MOVE ON!

Take the *parkour* or improv metaphors to heart! Watch these disciplines on video or, better yet, live. What can you learn from a *traceuse* or an improviser? Think about how you might introduce your team to these concepts. How is your workgroup responding to the offers and obstacles?

This week catch yourself in the act of holding your breath! Practice inhaling and exhaling. If you are like me, you will find this is not always as easy as it sounds. As you focus on it, you will be amazed at how often you are blocking the flow. Remind yourself in those moments to breathe!

The improvisation workshop was brilliant!

Alena threw herself into the scenes. She was a natural. "She trusts herself so much," thought Zoe. "Her confidence gives her the freedom to take a risk and even fail. She isn't worried about making a mistake. She is simply enjoying the process."

Zoe was absolutely captivated! One of the exercises was called, "Yes, and..." Clearly the object of this game was to build on the ideas of others—to add perspective, deepen the meaning, or give it a new spin.

The opening offer was a simple statement: "I had a strange dream last night." The second player embraced the offer with, "*Yes, and* do you remember the last time you had a strange dream?"

"*Yes, and* I still can't go near blueberry pie." The third player laughed, tossing the offer back with a twist.

The game went on and the story took off. It was amazing to see how those two little words—*yes* and *and*—impacted the story and the players. The scene was a creative collaboration, and it was energizing. Even when the players wanted to change the direction of the scene, they found ways to acknowledge the offer and redirect using the phrase, "Yes, and..."

Zoe thought about how many times she had responded to offers with the words, "No, but..." Those words have impact too. They block the flow, shut down communication, and damage trust. Different scenes played through her mind—conversations with her friends and family, work scenarios, and even conversations in her own head!

After watching a few more scenes, Zoe amazed herself by stepping onto the stage. She didn't plan to do this, but suddenly she was there!

At first she felt awkward and self-conscious, but as the scene advanced, she relaxed and allowed herself to focus on and accept the offers. The other players were more experienced than she was, and they encouraged her. If she missed an offer or didn't know how to proceed, they skillfully pushed the scene forward. She was taking a huge risk, but she felt very safe, surrounded by people who wanted her to win. It was exhilarating.

When she finished, there was spontaneous applause, and she spotted Alena, who was proudly giving her a standing ovation. Zoe laughed at that and took a little bow. She knew Alena wasn't applauding her performance. She was applauding the risk Zoe had taken and the obstacle she had overcome. She had accepted the offer of this experience. She had accepted, and she had responded.

Driving home, they were both exhausted. "That is a lot of work!" Alena laughed.

It was a lot of fun too. Zoe couldn't remember the last time she had laughed so much. "I really want to go again," she told Alena. "I learned so much, especially how to stay focused on my objective and share control with the other players. The experienced actors seemed to sense when I was struggling, and they knew how to help me through it."

"Those are great concepts for work. Sharing control is not always easy. Knowing when and how to assist a struggling player can also be a real challenge," Alena agreed. "The improvisers meet once a week, and I would love to go again too."

"In *parkour*, the players interact with obstacles in the environment to overcome them. I think improv works like that too. You must learn how to work with pieces you don't control to push the scene forward," Zoe observed. She was thinking aloud now. Alena seemed to understand that Zoe was working something out.

"Obstacles become resources for greater skill and creativity..." Zoe paused for a long time before finishing her thought, "...if you let them."

After a pause Alena said, "Yes, and I know you will let them. I'm going to be more aware of my offers. I think it might be easy to miss an offer if you're not paying attention."

At home, Zoe put up her feet and closed her eyes. Spontaneous lessons in *parkour* and improv were amazing ways to prepare for her one-hundred-day audition. "It is true," she thought. "If you seek answers, they will arrive wrapped in the most unusual packages."

She thought about how the experienced improvisers had skillfully helped her over the rough passages of the scene, and that reminded her of a C. S. Lewis quote her mother loved so much: "The next best thing to being wise oneself is to live in a circle of those who are."[8]

She concentrated on breathing in and out—giving and receiving, accepting and responding. She imagined overcoming obstacles and solving problems with grace and efficiency. In the corner of her mind, Zoe caught just a glimpse of wisdom. It was like an actor waiting in the wings and ready to take the stage. She whispered a prayer before drifting off to sleep.

seven

MAKE YOUR MOVES COUNT

Making a Real Difference in Real Time

Zoe hit the ground running with her one-hundred-day audition. It consisted of three client care phases: analysis to find the gaps, goals to fill them, and action steps to achieve the targets. After meeting with Alison several times, the plan was approved, and Alison asked her to present it at the next team meeting.

She prepared a simple one-page outline and made a copy for each team member. The real presentation she knew wasn't the handout. It would be the story she would tell. "This is incredible," Zoe thought as she planned her speaking points. "Just a few weeks ago, I was arranging chairs and ordering sandwiches for a meeting like this. Tomorrow I am on the agenda!"

The next morning Zoe arrived early. It was still dark outside, but the agency was fully lit, and there were several cars in the lot.

The team had been working around the clock on the new account. She knew they were under a great deal of pressure. She'd even heard a few stray comments

147

here and there about "biting off more than we can chew." Even Sara, who was normally so outgoing and friendly, seemed consumed by the pace and intensity of the project.

As they gathered for the meeting—most of them rushing into the room at the last minute, finishing conversations, and working on the run—Zoe admired their energy and focus. This really was an amazing group of people, and she was on the team! For at least one hundred days, she reminded herself.

Alison began the meeting by asking for updates on the new account and reviewing the project timelines. There were a few tasks running behind schedule, but the client was very pleased with the work they had done so far. Alison was "cautiously optimistic" about the progress and thanked everyone for their extraordinary commitment.

The next item on the agenda was Zoe's plan. Every eye in the room was fixed on her, and Zoe's voice trembled slightly as she began to speak.

"Since meeting all of you and learning about the new account, my challenge has been to find a way to support your efforts and add value. I think I've found a way to do that, and Alison as asked me to share my plan." With that Zoe distributed the outline.

"Before I walk through this plan, I want to tell you about two experiences that have changed my perspective. The first experience happened in a park, and the second on a stage. Both of them taught me how to interact more effectively with challenges, obstacles, and opportunities." Zoe went on to tell the story of her *parkour* and improv lessons, carefully weaving the metaphors together and tying them to her plan.

After telling the story, Zoe referenced the outline. "The goal is to increase the value we bring to existing clients. I want to find out how we can partner more effectively with them and work with you to address those opportunities."

The room was very quiet. Zoe wanted to think the group was captivated by her story, but it didn't feel like that at all. It was an awkward silence—the kind that makes you look for the nearest door.

She glanced at Todd across the conference room table. He actually had a snarl on his face. He was glaring at her, and she had no idea why. She looked to Sara for reassurance, but Sara would not meet her eyes.

Zoe felt like an intruder.

Alison quickly rescued her. "Thank you, Zoe, for the thought you have put into this plan." She looked around the room before continuing, "This team is stretched thin. I am proud of the work you are doing, and I am thrilled to have Zoe focusing on our long-time clients. We are reaching for more and holding on to what we have. Both strategies are critical, and I know I can count on every member of this team." She smiled reassuringly at Zoe before dashing off to her next commitment.

The meeting broke, and Zoe gathered her things. "Apparently the honeymoon is over," she thought as she walked back to her desk. Zoe wasn't sure what had just happened. It was as if she had run head-on into an invisible wall.

"That's going to leave a mark," the sarcastic voice chirped in her head.

"I feel like you are mining for flaws," Todd said sharply, interrupting her thoughts. "You are looking for what we haven't done or should have done differently. That concerns me, especially if you are giving our clients that impression. We have worked very hard to secure these accounts, and we've done great work for them. Your background hardly qualifies you to oversee my work."

Zoe was stunned. How in the world could he think her mission was to discover and highlight short-comings? What gave Todd the impression she was monitoring his performance? When she found her voice, she started to say, "No, that is not the message of this plan, but I do think there are ways to..." She stopped short, remembering the improvisation game. This was an offer! She needed to accept it and respond to it.

Taking a breath, Zoe gathered herself and said, "*Yes*, you have done exceptional work, *and* the intent of this plan is to protect and build on what you have created."

Now the offer was in Todd's court, and Zoe waited to see how he would respond. But Todd had not been to improv workshop. He didn't recognize or accept the offer. His response was intentionally rude. "You are the new girl here, Zoe. The accounts you are playing with don't belong to you." With that he turned and walked away.

CHECK YOUR LABEL

We are all wearing labels; these are also known as personal brands. Our character Zoe has worked very hard to design a powerful and positive brand. Painstakingly, she has unearthed what is unique and special about her. She has labored over the value she would deliver to the agency. For all of that, she was instantly labeled as "the new girl." (That tag came with her when she walked in the door of the agency.)

Zoe's problem isn't new. People who have decided to "jump the tracks," moving to a new role or discipline, face a similar challenge. The old position or title is a brand. It can be difficult to break through that and gain the respect and support you need in your new role.

Here's another challenge. Recently an executive told me, "I've worked very hard to change my brand, and I think I've actually succeeded. The problem is I'm not sure if I'm in love with the new one."

We both laughed as we talked about her very deliberate efforts to establish a brand that may not be exactly the one she wants. This executive definitely felt the new brand was more positive and powerful, but she wondered if it had really hit the mark. Will this brand inspire the trust and respect she will need to make the difference she wants to make?

These stories have me thinking:

- It's wise to think carefully about the brand you want to design. Think about it strategically, in the long term. Build a brand that supports the "future you."

- Rebranding is absolutely possible. If you are not happy with the brand you have, you have the power to change that.

- If you want to radically alter your brand, perhaps there are natural steps and phases. You can build a strong brand over time.

- The labels you carry are not just about you. People have preconceived notions based on the circumstances or the "scene." You may have to overcome a brand that was established before you arrived.

• Brands inspire feelings. They operate at an emotional level, and that's a good place to start in designing yours. What feelings do you want your brand to convey?

Author Robin Fisher Roffer gives us this objective for branding: "Your goal will be to let your brand become a vehicle for your most authentic self. In this way you'll distinguish yourself from others who do similar work, affirm your true identity, highlight your talents, and establish your reputation in business."[1]

Branding is intentional and deliberate. It is designing the label you want. Strong brands are forged over time with consistency. There is predictability to a good brand. People know what to expect. They expect it because that has been their experience over and over again.

Much of the work you've been doing (if you've been keeping up with the exercises) has prepared you to evaluate your brand. You have a strategy and vision of success. You have discovered things about yourself. You have also identified what you want and need from your work.

In many ways you have painted a portrait of your most authentic self. Branding is simply making those values, talents, and characteristics more visible and accessible to others.

What do people think when they hear your name? How do they feel? What's on your label? Is yours a name brand or generic? The most important question is: What do you want others to think, feel, and believe about you?

Once you have decided what you want the brand to be, look for ways to reinforce those attributes. Declare them!

Kris spent a great deal of time designing her strategy and her brand. When she completed a gap analysis, she found that her experiences were very tactical. Her boss relied on her to complete tasks, but he wasn't looking to her for recommendations and ideas. She wanted to be known as strategic and innovative, but the label said "dependable and thorough—someone I can count on to get things done."

"My work looked more like a grocery list," she confessed. "My boss didn't recognize the attributes I wanted him to see. That was impacting my ability to collect the experiences I needed to reach my long-term plan."

Kris began to focus on and declare her brand. "I literally announced it to my boss," she laughs. "I deliberately used the words *strategy* and *innovation*. I found ways to incorporate those terms in my conversations with him. I looked for ways to demonstrate my ability to think ahead, anticipating issues and opportunities. Before long, he was using those words to describe me! He started expecting me to be strategic and innovative. That has changed what he relies on me for and what I am working on."

Is this a branding miracle?

Not really. It is marketing, and that's what branding is all about. First you decide what you want the label to say. Then you speak and behave in ways that reinforce those attributes and values. *You advertise.*

PUBLIC SERVICE ANNOUNCEMENT

Look for behaviors that will undermine your brand. What are you doing (or not doing) that dilutes the brand, scatters the message, or confuses your customer?

Kris provided her boss with invisible cue cards. She prompted him to look for the attributes she wanted to showcase. She made her value more obvious, and that made her talents more accessible.

Over time, rather than saying, "I need you to..." Kris's boss said things like, "What do you think we can do about..."

I smile when I tell that story because even in this example, Kris was demonstrating what she wants to be known for. Her branding story is one of strategy and innovation.

As Zoe is learning, brands are important, because people use them to make decisions about what to buy or what not to buy, what to invest in, what to trust in, or what to believe. Think about that in the context of what you are offering. How is your brand helping or hindering your progress? How does it highlight your talents and distinguish you? How does it reflect your value?

LEARN HOW TO PRESENT YOUR VALUE MORE EFFECTIVELY

I've been evangelizing this point for years. Market yourself! Stop talking about what you do, and start talking about the difference you make. Sell the value of your work. Then I learned the lesson personally, in two acts, back to back. The lesson was frustrating and humbling and oh so timely.

The first installment of my lesson was a large conference. The room was filled with hundreds of people, and I gave that performance every ounce of my strength. I had a marvelous time with the group, and they rewarded me with a standing ovation. The air was electric, and the audience was energized. I stepped off the platform and headed for the book-signing table.

Ten people met me there. Ten! I kept waiting for the big line to show up. It didn't.

Later that evening we were debriefing the day as a team, trying to figure out what had happened. How can you have that kind of synergy with an audience and not generate more interest in the book?

We ran through a handy list of excuses: the economy, placement of the table, timing of presentation, and so on. My team was trying to encourage me, but I knew there was more to it. Then it hit me. I knew the secret.

I was breaking my own rule and doing the very thing I encourage women not to do. I had fallen into the "performance trap." In your head the performance trap sounds something like this: "If I just work hard enough and perform really, really well, people will like me, and they will see the value." There's only one problem with that theory. It isn't true, and dancing to that tune will wear out your shoes!

The next few days were frustrating. The problem was right in front of me, but the solution wasn't. I didn't know what to do about my performance problem. As if on cue, part two of my lesson arrived. This installment happened live on the radio.

Michael Ray Dresser is a fabulous radio host. He asks tough questions and really engages the audience. During the interview, I sensed he was reaching for something. He was managing the message differently, and I was having a hard time keeping up. I felt off balance and out of sync.

I was surprised when Michael Ray called me the next day. Here's what he said: "Thank you for the interview. I have some feedback for you. Would you like to hear it?"

Alarms went off in my head (but of course I said yes).

He continued, "People like you. You're likable and you're smart. You have a good message." (At this point I was feeling pretty good about me.) That bubble burst when he said, "The people who need your book, the people you write for, will not buy your book because they like you. They will buy your book because it is the solution they need and the answer they are searching for. Liking you is not the point. It has never been the point. It really isn't about you at all."

After letting that sink in a bit, Michael Ray told me a story about the millions of people who bought quarter-inch drill bits last year. Not one of them needed or wanted a quarter-inch drill bit. All of them wanted a quarter-inch hole!

The point landed. I was selling drill bits, and people don't buy drill bits. People buy holes. They buy solutions.

Over the next few weeks, Michael Ray coached me. He put me through the ropes of managing my message and telling my story more effectively. He challenged my perspective and capabilities. It has been a rigorous and wonderful process. It has changed the way I write and the way I present. It has helped me connect at a new level with my clients. After talking about it for years, I am learning how to present solutions in a more meaningful way. I am learning how to frame my work with value.

If that sounds like a sales message, it is. You may not think of yourself as being in sales. If that is true, I hope you will reconsider. We are all salespeople! We have solutions and ideas "for sale." We must sell the boss on the resources we need or the projects we want to work on. We promote our skills and capabilities. We sell "us."

If you "buy" this notion, what needs to change about the way you tell the story and talk about your value? What exactly are you the solution to? How can you present your work in a frame of value? How can you turn even frustrating scenarios into wins for you and for others?

CREATE MORE WINS WITH YOUR NEGOTIATIONS

Pam is one of the brightest, most strategic people I have ever met. Honestly, I think she is brilliant. She sees what others miss. She spots patterns, trends, and consequences others overlook. Pam is genuinely committed to her team and to the goals of the organization. She is unconcerned with "who gets credit" for the work. "As long as we get the result," she told me, "I don't care who gets the badge of honor."

I smiled when she said that. Pam is working in an industry that has typically been populated by men. (Some of you are smiling now too, thinking, "Which of us isn't?") That's not a problem for her either; she has established solid working relationships throughout the organization. She looks for the best in everyone. Even when they "behave badly," she assumes their intentions were admirable. She expects the best from her boss, colleagues, and direct reports.

She pushes others to the front and gives them the spotlight. She involves her business partners and generously shares her insights. When her boss or peers "miss" something important, Pam has a marvelous way of "fixing" it and making it seem like it was someone else's idea! (I told you she's brilliant.)

So what's the problem? Pam is talented, committed, and builds good working relationships. All of that looks good on the surface, but if you dig down just a bit, you will find the issue. People step over her, make decisions without consulting her, and take credit for her work (even at very high levels of the organization). Apparently not everyone is unconcerned with who gets the credit!

After Pam had shared several examples and scenarios with me, the pattern became very clear. Pam was empowering, promoting, and protecting everyone but herself. As she had so graciously moved backstage and taken a supporting role, it was damaging her credibility and "influence-ability." We talked about that for a while and decided on two things:

1. This isn't about competing for attention or jock-
   eying for position. We don't have to take the credit
   or spotlight from others. It's important that we
   empower people and highlight the achievements of

others. The secret is to create those moments for you too.

2. The scenarios Pam presented as examples were all negotiations. Every one of them was an opportunity to negotiate for what she needed to be more confident, successful, respected, and satisfied in her role.

Once Pam reframed the troubling situations as negotiations, her answers appeared. *She discovered that in each if these negotiations, she was creating the win for others without creating a win for herself.* Viewing the scenarios as real negotiations gave Pam "permission" to win also; it was then easy for her to talk about what she needed. "I want to be involved in the decisions that impact my team. I want the people who work for and with me to understand and respect my role. I want us to work together without undermining each other even unintentionally."

There is absolutely nothing wrong with setting others up for the win. Do more of that! And while you're at it, invite yourself to the party. Learn to create wins for yourself too. There really is enough success to go around.

Looking for and creating more wins will set you apart. These are the defining moves. Sometimes you'll find the solutions inside your department or company, but it's also important to look beyond those borders. The answer you're looking for may not be "in the house."

LOOK BEYOND YOUR EXPERIENCE AND THE BOUNDARIES OF YOUR ORGANIZATION TO MAKE THINGS BETTER

Most of the organizations I work with are looking for ways to do things faster and better at less cost. From a project management perspective, that's pushing on three constraints simultaneously—

time, money, and quality. That's difficult to do, because these elements impact each other.

If we do it faster, we may give on quality. If we focus on quality, it may take more time. If we cut the cost or dedicate fewer resources, time and quality may be affected. It's a frustrating circle, and it can spin you around until you're dizzy.

Sometimes the answer is "in the house." We can find a way to make things better internally by improving a process, eliminating unnecessary steps, strengthening skills, and so on. We can innovate internally to improve (and we should always be looking for ways to do that).

We can also look outside of our walls to find solutions.

- How can you leverage vendors and service providers more effectively? Are you asking them to innovate? Are you drawing from their experience across industries and organizations?

- What are other companies doing to attack the issues you face?

- Where will you find the next generation of ideas?

These questions ask us to look beyond our boundaries to find new ideas and solutions. Good news! You don't have to have all of the answers.

Chloe certainly found this to be true. As a training coordinator for a government agency, she was challenged by a shortfall in funding. Cuts across the organization hit her department hard. Initially, she looked for ways to deliver training less expensively. All the frills were gone. No more beverages or snacks. Even pens were eliminated.

"There's only so much you can cut," Chloe tells me as she

shares her story. "Once I had exhausted those measures, I had to innovate."

Chloe reviewed the training calendar and canceled classes that were poorly attended, but she still had to find a way to meet her training objectives within the constraints of her new budget. "I turned to my vendors," she recalls. "I picked up the phone and asked them what other organizations were doing to manage cost while still delivering quality training."

The advice she received was valuable. Chloe learned that some organizations were moving select courses to a webinar format—training delivered via the phone and Internet. She also discovered the ability to co-op training—sharing resources with other agencies around the city.

"Instead of paying a speaker to deliver a workshop for our agency alone, we looked for opportunities to share the expense. That meant we could deliver a high-quality seminar at less expense. Those were also great networking events. People had the opportunity to meet peers and colleagues from other agencies. We leveraged that as a deliberate strategy and built networking into the format of the workshops. This was so successful that we wondered why we hadn't thought of it before. Sometimes adversity really does pay off!"

These are just a few of the ideas Chloe unearthed as she searched for solutions beyond her borders. "Even having the conversation with vendors was beneficial," Chloe says. "Our service providers understood the constraints and worked with us to find solutions. They knew this was not just my problem, but it was *our* problem."

What began as a budgeting nightmare became an exercise in innovation. Chloe would tell you it was a rigorous and rewarding exercise. "The quality of training actually improved," she tells me. "And I found my team! There were training coordinators all over the state wrestling with the same issues. I tapped into that need. A group of us meet regularly by phone to work through the challenges and share ideas. Those relationships have been like striking gold."

Chloe's story underscores the value of negotiating, networking, and even masterminding. She is building her brand and delivering tangible value. She is giving and receiving. She accepted the offer and moved the scene forward, overcoming the obstacles like a skilled *traceuse*. Her example also shows us how it is possible to manage and influence things we don't control.

MANAGING UP AND OVER TO MOVE AHEAD

Something marvelous happens when we realize we can influence people and situations we do not personally control. Our title may not say manager, but each of us has the opportunity to manage up and over to move ahead. We can influence decision makers and the people we count on to achieve results.

Managing up refers to the situations and people above us in the organization. Managing over is influencing people and circumstances across the organization. These people don't report to us, and they don't have to cooperate with our plans. Situations may be completely out of our control, as in Chloe's case with the budget cuts.

Even so I find the most remarkable examples of people who have found a way to navigate those barriers with incredible grace. They don't rely on making people do anything, because they have learned how to create the *want to*. They work for commitment rather than compliance. They seek authentic buy-in, which is always achieved through involvement.

This is exactly where we find Zoe. She is learning that she can't make the team participate in her plan. She must find a way to influence what they think and how they feel about it. She will need to involve the people who are impacted by her plan and turn them into shareholders or owners.

GET YOUR MOVE ON!

Brands are forged at an emotional level. They make people feel special. They deliver on a promise, inspire confidence, and signal value. My favorite brands have established that unique, one-of-a-kind impression. I feel special when I use these products and do business with these companies.

This week, focus on your brand in order to understand what the labels are versus what you would like them to be. If you suspect yours is a "generic" brand, search for ways to distinguish yourself. I suspect you will find the answers in how people feel when they are doing business with you.

Find a way to add value by making something work better or cost less. As you make those recommendations or implement your ideas, plan to involve others. Especially when the work you are doing introduces change, find ways to include the people who will be impacted. Involvement is a universal key that will unlock the door to cooperation and commitment.

Todd's remarks had indeed left their mark. His parting words, "You're the *new girl*, Zoe," stuck in her brain and played over and over like an annoying tune she couldn't get out of her head.

To compound the agony, no one except Todd spoke to her after the meeting. Alison wasn't available to meet with her, and the team was consumed with the new account. Everyone disappeared behind a curtain of quiet conferences and project plans. All of this left Zoe feeling like an unwelcome guest at dinner.

She literally dragged herself through the day, wondering if five o'clock would ever come. All enthusiasm had drained from the plan. She could barely bring herself to look at it, let alone work on it. When the clock finally released her, she grabbed her coat and bolted for freedom.

"What steps did you take to prepare your plan?" Alena asked after Zoe told her the gruesome story over the phone that evening.

"I'm not sure what you mean exactly," Zoe admitted. She was curled up in the corner of her couch, dangerously close to a fetal position. "I reviewed my notes from the original team meeting, found my niche, and looked for the need I could fill and the value I could offer. From there I built an outline and presented it to Alison."

Alena thought about that for a moment before asking, "Is there such thing as too much initiative, Zoe?"

"Absolutely not," Zoe blurted out. "You can never, ever show too much initiative!"

Alena was smiling. Zoe could hear it in her voice when she said, "If there were such a thing, Zoe, what would it look like?"

Zoe could feel Alena reaching right through the phone to pull something from her. She was still groping for an answer when Alena offered a hint. "Maybe it will help if we back up a step. What does initiative look like?"

This reminded Zoe of the improv workshop when she had been hopelessly stuck and the other actors had helped her advance the scene. "Initiative is taking action. It is ambition and moxie and drive," Zoe listed. "It is inventiveness and innovation. It is what I tried to demonstrate with this plan." Silently Zoe continued her list. "It's a major word on my storyboard! It's what I was totally missing on my last job, and that's why I am on the phone now trying to answer another really hard question. I've been thrown into the question time-out again!"

"Now we are getting somewhere," Alena reassured her. "Initiative is all of those things. But what if those things were overdone? What if there was too much drive and too much moxie? What would that look like?"

Zoe sighed. "Well," she said slowly, as the answer emerged, "if I were absolutely required to describe too much initiative, I would say it looks aggressive, like driving right over people, rushing ahead, and being too eager."

There was a long pause on the line.

"Is it possible that you have somehow driven over people in your eagerness to demonstrate value?" Alena brought the point home.

"If that is true, why didn't Alison say something?" Zoe objected. "I presented my plan to her more than once. She offered suggestions. I wish she would have told me. I feel like she deliberately let me run into a wall." Visions of *parkour* mishaps flooded her brain. These pictures weren't at all helpful.

"Perhaps she assumed you had included the team in building your plan, or maybe she missed it," Alena answered patiently. "There's another possibility too. Perhaps she trusts you with this opportunity to grow. How would you feel if you believed she trusted you with learning this lesson in real time?"

Zoe considered those possibilities for a moment. She was thinking about one of the improv fundamentals: you may need to change your approach, but you must keep your eye on the objective.

"If your plan isn't working, you have the power to change that," Alena said, breaking the silence. "Don't be surprised or disappointed to learn that in addition to managing your assignments and projects, you must also manage up, which means managing the expectations and even the direction and feedback you receive from your boss. It's important to take charge of that. You have the power to take responsibility for managing the resources you need to do your job. You also have to manage over. That means partnering across the organization to achieve the results you are looking for."

Zoe was spent. "That's a whole lot to wrap my arms around, Alena. I didn't see this coming. I thought the team would be thrilled with my plan to support the clients they have worked so hard to land. Instead they see me as a thief coming to take charge of something that isn't mine."

"Ah, now you're talking about ownership," Alena said. "Today this is your plan, and you've encountered resistance. I know you are looking for a fast win. You want to put an early success on the scoreboard. What if you decided to create the win by creating more winners? How would that change your plan?"

There was a long pause as Zoe struggled for the answer. Alena was seeing something she did not, and Zoe knew her mentor would not rush the process by providing the solution. This was a woman who firmly believed each person is responsible for the search and the discovery.

Suddenly it clicked! Zoe could see and even understand the team's reaction to her plan. She had not included them. She had carved out a niche all right, and it had cut deeply into their sense of ownership and control. She had taken over the scene without thinking about the other actors. How could she have missed that?

After saying good night to Alena, Zoe opened her laptop and added the word *catalyst* to the storyboard. "I will be a catalyst for results," she told Minnie. "Rather than presenting a plan, I'll open the dialogue. I'll be the spark, igniting positive action."

When she arrived at the agency the next morning, she hung up her coat and walked resolutely to Todd's office. He was there, looking very weary. She wondered if he'd slept at all. Surely the hours and pressure had something to do with his reaction to the plan.

"Todd," Zoe said firmly, "when you have time today, I'd appreciate a few moments."

"It's probably now or never, Zoe," he said in a resigned way. "Today is fully loaded."

166

She sat across the desk from him and leaned forward to underscore the words. "The feedback you gave me yesterday was very difficult." Todd started to interrupt, but she held up her hand to stop him. "Please, let me finish. I worked very hard on that plan, and I was excited to present it to the team—my team. Even so, I missed something very important. I am here to support all of you and our clients. I am here to add value, and in my rush to do that, I forgot to ask you what you need."

Zoe straightened herself, bracing for a response. She was shaking inside. That had not been easy to say. She felt terribly vulnerable and exposed.

Todd leaned back in his chair. The child in Zoe hoped just a little that he would tip right over, but he didn't.

He took a long time to answer, and Zoe was determined not to interrupt the silence. Finally he said, "The plan took me off guard, Zoe. I felt blindsided. While I can't speak for the team, I don't think I was alone in feeling that way. I was very hard on you yesterday, and there's no excuse for that. I reacted badly, and I'm sorry."

Todd's apology was an offer, and Zoe was determined to advance the scene. "*Yes*, you were very hard on me, *and* I appreciate the feedback," she replied. "The thing is, the feedback you've given me tells me what you don't want or need." Zoe smiled then to lighten the moment. "I'm pretty clear on those points. What I'm here to learn is how I can help. Will you help me revise the plan?"

With the few moments Todd could spare, they reviewed the plan together. He made several recommendations, and she could feel his resistance fading. She also found real merit in his advice. She committed to the changes and asked for an appointment the following day to follow up. In the meantime, she told Todd she intended to meet with the other team members. "I want this to be our plan," she confided. "This can be a win for everyone on the team."

At the door, Zoe turned to say, "Todd, can we agree that you will never call me the 'new girl' again?"

His face turned the most amazing shade of red! "Yes," he said, crossing his heart. "I give you my word."

With that settled, Zoe gathered up every ounce of her remaining moxie and went to work.

eight

EXIT SIGNS

When You Have to Go in Order to Grow

As promised, Zoe met with each of the team members for a needs assessment, and the plan came to life. Not only were her action steps clear, but they were also clearly valued. She had come into this looking for a fast win, and she had found one: to understand the needs of her team and demonstrate the ability to meet those needs.

The clients won too, and the one hundred days flew by.

The new account continued to be a challenge. As Alison predicted, this client was very demanding, and resources were stretched dangerously thin. Skills were pushed too. The team referred to the new account as "the mountain" because the learning curve was steep and they felt like they were moving a mountain, one boulder at a time.

Stress charged a heavy toll. The fabric of the team was severely tested, and at times it threatened to tear. It was at one of these moments Zoe suggested an improv workshop to coax everyone out of the office and regain perspective. After some not-so-gentle nudging by Alison, the group wearily agreed.

It was a fantastic night. The team is still talking about that experience. It gave them a common lexicon. It's not unusual now to hear someone at the agency say, "Let's advance this scene" or "You're blocking my offer!" For the first time in weeks they were laughing and relaxing.

After that, things seemed to even out, with the exception of Sara, who was really struggling in her role. Over time, she became one of the greatest obstacles the team encountered. She was critical, distant, and passive, with episodes of unexplained defensiveness that reminded Zoe of a cornered animal.

"This project has changed her," Zoe thought. "I don't even recognize her anymore." She remembered the first time she'd seen Sara. She was smiling warmly and welcoming Zoe to the agency. Sara hadn't smiled like that in a very long time.

Zoe concentrated on using "yes and..." each time Sara resisted and objected. She was determined to view these interactions as offers, and she tried very hard to help Sara advance the scene. Her efforts were not successful. Sara seemed equally determined to be an obstacle. In a team meeting the final blow landed.

Todd asked Sara for an update on an overdue task. She glared at him coldly, stood, and walked out of the meeting without a word. After a brief meeting with Alison, Sara packed her personal things and left the agency without saying good-bye.

"Sara and I have agreed this is no longer a good fit," Alison told the team later in the day. There was sadness in her eyes and her voice. Nothing more needed to be said.

Zoe thought about calling Sara or sending a note. "Perhaps I can reach out to her the way Alena reached out to me," she thought. After several attempts with no response, Zoe understood that Sara was not looking for a lifeline or a friend. She had walked out the door and closed it firmly behind her.

A few days later Alison asked to meet Zoe over lunch. The one-hundred-day audition was coming to a close. Zoe was proud of her accomplishments, but as she unfolded her napkin, her hands were visibly trembling.

"I want to thank you, Zoe, for the work you've done and the value you've created," Alison jumped right in. "You've executed the plan well and helped us through a very challenging time."

Zoe's heart dropped. That sounded a lot like, "Thanks so much, and that'll be all. OK, bye-bye now." She couldn't hide the disappointment in her face, and she dared not meet Alison's eyes. If only they weren't at lunch! How would she make it through a farewell meal?

Twisting her napkin under the table, Zoe finally found her voice. "Thank you, Alison, for the opportunity. This has been a wonderful experience. I've learned so much."

"Your goal to become indispensable to the team happened more quickly than you may have imagined," Alison said smiling. If she'd noticed Zoe's heartbreak, she wasn't letting on. "I'd like to discuss a new role with the agency. The team wholeheartedly agrees, and I hope you will too."

It took a few seconds for that to sink in. A new role with the agency! This was not an exit; it was an encore! She had auditioned and won the part!

"I'd love to hear more about that opportunity," Zoe said enthusiastically. "I've become quite attached to this team and to our clients."

So it was. Over lunch Alison described the position she envisioned for Zoe. It was a bigger job to be sure: account manager. There would be a lot to learn, and she would need to come up to speed quickly. Alison also asked Zoe to mentor a new team member. "As you transition into your new role, I will need someone to take your place. You've created a valuable niche, Zoe, and I don't want that to become a gaping hole."

The idea of mentoring someone excited Zoe. "I would love to be a mentor," she told Alison. That reminded Zoe of her own mentor. She could hardly wait to tell Alena the news. But she would tell the windshield first, of course. It was always the first to know.

MAKE YOUR TRANSITIONS SUCCESSFUL BY REACHING FOR, RATHER THAN RUNNING FROM, SOMETHING

It's so uncomfortable to be uncomfortable. When we are in pain, the first instinct is to make the pain stop! The problem with this approach is that we can make ourselves feel better by treating symptoms without solving real issues. We miss valuable opportunities to grow.

More than once I've watched people pack up and leave a situation with their problems faithfully tagging along behind. They bring old, tattered baggage to bright new opportunities, superimposing the past onto the future. (Honestly, how tragic is that?)

I am a firm believer that lessons not learned will be repeated. Cindy is a good example. Everywhere Cindy goes, she is overworked, taken advantage of, and terribly mistreated. That just makes me want to say, "*Hmmm.*"

Cindy will tell you that all of her bosses have been incompetent boars and most of her co-workers are gossiping shrews, jealous of anyone with half a brain. (That is dangerously close to a quote.)

The only common denominator in these scenarios is (you guessed it) Cindy. When I ever-so-gently pointed that out, there was a definite push back. Cindy became very defensive. Instantly I joined the ranks of people who don't understand and who want to see her fail. She wasn't ready to confront herself, so I invited to her to call me again if that changed.

No matter how miserable we are in the current place, I believe it's important to reach for rather than run from something. Sometimes moving signs do point toward the exit. It really is time to go. Sometimes that isn't the answer at all.

Discontent may be urging us to move out of a mundane routine and shake things up with innovation and creativity. Or perhaps the dissatisfaction we are experiencing is a wake-up call. (In that case, you really don't want to hit the snooze button.) Before packing it in, isolate the issues and define the problems. Otherwise you risk repeating the cycle in your next position.

Isolating the problem is another way of saying, "Where does it hurt?" Perhaps you like the work but not the people you work with. Or maybe it's the other way around. The people are great, but the work is not rewarding. Professor Edwin Locke, an American psychologist and thought leader in motivation and job satisfaction, gives us two dimensions of job satisfaction: conditions and agents.[1]

Conditions relate to the work itself, rewards, and context. Is the work challenging, interesting, and fulfilling? Can I succeed at this? Am I rewarded appropriately? How do hours, location, space, and other working conditions impact the attitude I have about my job? Even tools, technology, and equipment impact job satisfaction.

Agents are the people who influence the way we feel about our work. This includes your manager, colleagues, customers, and even your family. Do you work with talented, committed people? Is your manager supportive? Do you feel recognized and valued? What are your customers like? Does your family understand your work and support your efforts?

FOCUS ON THE PIECES YOU CAN INFLUENCE OR CONTROL

If we can isolate the pain points, we may have the opportunity to negotiate for the changes we need to feel better. Empower yourself in this process by focusing on the pieces you can influence or control. For example:

- If you are overwhelmed with your workload, you can look for ways to be more efficient and ask your boss to assist you in establishing more realistic deadlines and priorities.

- When the work is no longer challenging, you can ask for a special assignment or the opportunity to cross train and learn a new role.

- If hours are the issue, perhaps there is a way to put more flexibility in your schedule. Many organizations are open to the idea of flextime and telecommuting options allowing you to work from home part of the time. Make this case by demonstrating benefits for the organization and for you. These arrangements clearly need to be win-wins.

- For colleague problems, think about the boundaries you've established and the way you handle conflict. How are you contributing to the problem? (Each time I have mustered up the courage to ask that big, grown-up question, the answers have surprised me.)

- If your job includes working through difficult customer situations, you may need to find better ways to manage the stress or develop new skills and strategies.

This list does not come with a guarantee. You may do the work suggested here and arrive at the conclusion it really is time to leave. I hope you will do the work anyway. Whether you stay or go, this process demonstrates personal accountability, and it reduces the chances that you will have to repeat a painful cycle to learn a valuable lesson.

WHEN IS IT TIME TO CALL IT QUITS?

You've probably heard this motivational quote attributed to Vince Lombardi: "Quitters never win and winners never quit." I believed that for the longest time. It was almost heresy for me to even consider quitting!

Through some very difficult personal and professional experiences, I have learned that winners do quit! More importantly, they know what and when to quit. One of my favorite authors, Seth Godin, puts it this way, "Quit the wrong stuff. Stick with the right stuff. Have the guts to do one or the other."[2]

I've been through this cycle with jobs and relationships, ideas and plans. It is excruciating. I would gather every ounce of my resolve and press on no matter what until I reached the very end of myself. Then gently God would peel my fingers off this thing I had been clutching so tightly. Without the strength to resist, I would finally release. You would think I'd have learned more quickly how to quit or least how to distinguish (in Godin's terms) a dip from a dead end.

What is the difference? Dips are the valleys that grow you up, challenge you, build endurance, and shape you for success. Dead ends are the cul-de-sacs that wear you down, steal your confidence, and rob you of your vision.

Valleys are good for us. While not a walk in the park, they beg us to grow. Dead ends are just loops. You don't get through them; you just keep going around (and in my experience, with every circle, you lose a little more of yourself until you are unrecognizable).

Be strategic even with your quitting. This is a decision, not an emotion. Feelings don't make very good deciders. There is room for logic and creativity as you explore your options. (And you do have options.) No matter how stuck you feel, trust me, you aren't.

Most decision-making and problem-solving models include a sequence of steps.

1. Define the problem. Remember, if the problem isn't clear, the solutions will be muddy too.

2. Generate alternatives. From the obvious to the ridiculous, what are your choices as they relate to your circumstances and your goals?

3. Evaluate your options. This part can be a little tricky. To make an effective decision, you'll need criteria to score or rank your options. (You might refer to Locke's conditions and agents to create your criteria.)

4. In the model below, three options are evaluated, using a score of 1 as low to 5 as high. In this example, factors are also weighted, with quality of life carrying the highest value. Option 3 earns the highest score.

	Quality of Life: 80 percent	Challenge: 40 percent	Opportunity: 60 percent	Compensation: 50 percent	Total Score
Option 1	2 x .80 = 1.60	4 x .40 =1.60	5 x .60 = 3.00	3 x .50 = 1.50	**7.70**
Option 2	5 x .80 = 4.00	2 x .40 = .80	3 x .60 = 1.80	1 x .50 = .50	**7.10**
Option 3	3 x .80 = 2.40	4 x .40 = 1.60	5 x .60 = 3.00	2 x .50 = 1.00	**8.00**

5. Decide and implement. This step assumes a commitment and an action plan.

In addition to these steps, many of the tools we've already explored will assist you in solving problems and making wise decisions: mentoring, Mind Maps, gap analysis, and even journaling. Each of these will help you hold your choices to the light and see them from new perspectives.

PUBLIC SERVICE ANNOUNCEMENT

Remember, *no decision is a decision.* If you choose to do nothing, you have still chosen.

If you choose to do nothing, you must at least own your choice. Otherwise you fall prey to a victim mentality, and that is not an attractive brand! You are not a victim!

EXITS NEED A STRATEGY TOO

There's a ton of information out there about how to hunt for and land your next job. The "How to Quit With Class" section of the reference shelf is less populated. Ultimately, how you exit matters too. Be strategic about that because it becomes part of your brand.

This tends to be a very small world after all. Sometimes hasty exits bar future doors. We've all heard the saying, "Don't burn your bridges." That's really good advice, especially in today's workforce.

Hopefully all of your exits represent goals achieved, bold moves, and next steps. Even if (especially if) your decision to leave comes from a painful place, you'll want to get your strategy on. Think of it this way: everyone you work with is a potential endorsement or a potential barrier in the future.

I've seen it happen more than once—a bright new opportunity crushed by a former co-worker who put in a bad word behind the scenes. I've also watched the reverse—a résumé instantly relocated to the top of the stack after a recommendation from a past colleague.

Some people leave without a word, and others insist on having the last word. If they've been unhappy on the job, quitting seems like the perfect opportunity to make that oh so clear. I think both of these extremes miss the point all together. You really can build your brand all the way out the door.

One of the best pieces of advice I've heard on this topic is to make your exit about you and not about others or the organization. This is a beautiful way of owning your decision and making a good choice for yourself. That is powerful!

Along those lines, do what you can to leave the organization better than you found it. Help your team prepare for your departure. This goes beyond the two-week notice most employees offer as they tender a resignation. This is a proactive plan to help your employer succeed without you. If you are even slightly disgruntled, this is going to take every ounce of your personal discipline and integrity. You won't feel like helping. You will feel like making a point.

Kim had other plans when she left her last job. "I hope they fall apart when I leave," she announced proudly. "They haven't appreciated the work I do, and they are about to find out how valuable I really am."

178

That isn't a strategy; it's sabotage!

Below are seven tips from people who have made even the most difficult transitions with incredible grace and poise. This is good advice from classy people.

1. In the right time and the right way, tell your boss first! Do it in person whenever possible. If distance is an issue, pick up the phone. This is not the time for an e-mail with "My Resignation" in the subject line.

2. If things have been difficult, partner with your boss to frame the announcement. Get on the same page. This takes guessing and gossip out of the equation and allows the team to focus on the business mission.

3. After the announcement, contact the people who rely on you. Think about how your absence will impact them, and assist with the transition.

4. Leave checklists or instructions for tasks only you know how to do. You may even offer to be available (for a short period of time) for questions.

5. Refuse to catch "short-timer" syndrome. As long as you are collecting a check, earn it. Bring real value to the organization until it is time to go.

6. Bite your lip and tongue if necessary. Do not leave with a negative commentary about the company or anyone in it. Be especially cautious with the exit interview! Who knows in this crazy world? Someday you may actually want to come back, so don't slam any doors on your way out.

7. Make it easy for people to stay in touch. Quit your job, not your network.

Ideas like these will help you formulate your own exit strategy, one that is relevant to you and your situation. The most important point here is to be intentional with both your decisions and your actions. Make them part of a grander plan.

GET YOUR MOVE ON!

If you are considering a career change, or if you've been thrown into that pool by a change within your organization, develop a strategy for your exit. How you go speaks volumes about who you are. If the situation has been difficult, closure will come more quickly with a graceful good-bye.

Zoe was enjoying a long, lazy Saturday until the phone rang. The sound of it annoyed her, and she was tempted to ignore it—really, really tempted. The haranguing persisted until Minnie woke just enough to raise her head and throw a disapproving look. Zoe put the book down and managed a cheerful hello.

It was Madeline, and something was seriously up.

Her long-time friend was normally full of energy, endlessly optimistic, with opinions on pretty much everything. She was outspoken to the point of bossy, and for all of that Zoe adored her. Madeline had been strangely distant for the past several weeks. Zoe had assumed they were both just very busy. Obviously there was more.

Her voice was almost timid when Maddy asked, "Can I come over? I need to talk."

A few hours later Madeline was sitting statue straight on the edge of her chair and biting her lip to hold back the tears.

"I am utterly lost," she declared almost immediately. "I don't even know who I am anymore."

Zoe was stunned. How could Madeline, an absolute force of nature, feel this way? Taking a cue from Alena, who was brilliant in these "I've lost myself" situations, Zoe left the silence alone.

"I quit my job three weeks ago. My family needs me, and my job was consuming. It was the right decision. I didn't tell you or anyone really. I didn't even know how to explain." Madeline was speaking in choppy sound bites. Zoe knew that was her way of controlling the emotion in her voice.

This was big news. Madeline had been on a career fast track, taking two stairs at a time on her way to an executive position. "Tell me about it now," Zoe encouraged her.

"There's no drama really. The decision wasn't even difficult. My family comes first. The hard part happened when I realized my job was my identity. I left my job, and now I can't find me."

Zoe was in unfamiliar territory here. Usually Madeline was giving advice—welcome or not. Maddy was one of those people who process externally, thinking aloud and arriving at very firm convictions.

"You made a decision based on your values, Madeline. That takes courage. I am proud of you."

Madeline wasn't ready to hear that, but there was no anger in her voice when she answered. "Don't be proud of me. You're the one with the big, exciting job. The only thing I'm in charge of now is laundry, homework, and lunch boxes. The biggest decision I made yesterday was food related. I feel isolated. Zoe, I had no idea how much my job defined me."

"It sounds like you haven't fully accepted the position you've applied for." Zoe smiled reassuringly. "How will you redefine yourself in this new role?"

"I have no idea what that means, Zoe." Madeline rolled her eyes but seemed to be relaxing a bit. She sat back in the chair and took a deep breath. Thank goodness. Zoe was getting stiff just looking at her.

"It means," Zoe answered, matching Madeline's direct cadence, "you have taken on a new challenge. You have a big job with important customers, also known as your family. Every day you have the opportunity to bring the best of who you are to this role. You haven't lost your skills. You'll use them differently to achieve your goals. So, what exactly are you going to do with this opportunity? What is the difference you will make in this season of your life? How will you help your customers succeed?"

Now it was Madeline's turn to be stunned.

"While you're thinking about that, I'll make coffee," Zoe said as she marched from the room thinking how nice it was to finally put someone else in a "question time-out."

When she returned with two mugs, Madeline seemed to have found a bit of her balance. "Tell me something," she said. "When did my best friend become so wise?"

Zoe smiled at her and said, "When a really wise woman asked me three very hard questions."

nine

INSPIRING MOVES

You Were Destined for More

The episode with Madeline left Zoe exhilarated and exhausted. "Now I know how Alena feels after an appointment with me," she told Minnie, who was otherwise occupied studying a bird through the window.

She and Madeline had spent the afternoon designing a storyboard for Maddy's new role. They talked about the importance of staying connected, involved, and challenged.

At one point, Madeline became quite animated about the possibility of creating resources for women working at home or from home. The idea seemed to ignite something in her. Zoe recognized the look in her friend's eye. It said, "This is a project that can consume me and make me feel valuable."

"Maddy," Zoe said, searching for the right words, "I have no doubt you would be a brilliant resource and mentor; that may be exactly what you are called to do. How important is it to nail the job you have before you reach for more? How will your customers be impacted by this idea? What is your primary goal?"

Zoe braced herself for the fireworks by looking Madeline squarely in the eye. "You are absolutely right," Madeline sighed. Then she smiled. "What's with the three question thing?"

"Not sure," Zoe said munching a cookie. "Somehow the best questions seem to come in threes."

Armed with her vision and the glimpses of her new brand, Madeline had gone home to her precious "customers." Zoe smiled as she predicted how Madeline would not only accept the job but also excel in this new role.

"She's going to be fine," Zoe reassured Minnie. "Transitions are tough; they challenge you to the very core. If you allow them, they will show you who you are and what you are really capable of."

Suddenly it dawned on her. Everything she had recently been through had prepared her for this appointment with Madeline. There had been a greater purpose for her struggle, something beyond her. "Imagine that! It isn't all about me after all," she laughed.

Minnie rose, stretched, and sashayed out of the room. She flicked her tail for good measure. Zoe may have imagined the wink.

MANAGE YOUR TALENT

Much of the work I do revolves around talent management. I love this discipline because people are talent. Managing talent is to discover, develop, and leverage the human asset. It is drawing the possibility out. You are not an observer in this process; you are the actor.

Organizations use many models to assess and manage talent. Two factors—performance and potential—are often used to identify where talent lives and what can be done to maximize it. That means individuals are evaluated on how well they are performing in their current role and how much potential they have to move ahead.

Top performers who show strong potential are likely candidates for accelerated development. These are the rising stars—the people organizations want to retain and grow.

The performance part is pretty straightforward. Are you doing your job well? Are you taking good care of what is already yours? Have you nailed your job? This is the stuff performance reviews are made of, and we are used to thinking about our "scores" in this way.

The potential piece is harder to wrap your head around. How exactly do you measure a person's potential? Maybe the better question is, "How does one demonstrate potential, so she will stand out in the crowd?"

By definition, potential is "capable of being or becoming." Your potential, then, is what you are capable of being or becoming. The challenge is to understand your possibility and make it obvious and visible. Here are some ways to do that:

1. Have a career plan in place. The most successful people do. They know where they want to go, and they are making deliberate strides in that direction.

2. Share your goals and ask for the meaningful experiences that will allow you to prepare for the role you want to play.

3. Demonstrate extreme initiative and personal leadership. Look for ways to make a greater difference and become more of a resource.

These steps point directly to your high-performance zone. Managing the four elements (perspective, leadership, capabilities, and resources) allows you to recognize, develop, and market your highest potential.

Keep in mind that potential is both personal and situational. In other words, there is potential within you and within your circumstances. You need to unearth what is in and around you. You have to mine for it!

Here's another way to think about it: there is potential in a seed. Seeds don't look like much, but what they contain—the power they have to burst forth—is amazing. The same is true with you. The potential within you and around you is nothing short of amazing. (You may want to read that line ten more times and make it your personal declaration.)

FIND YOUR PURPOSE TO FIND YOUR POSSIBILITY

As I think about this, I am inclined to say, "Surely possibility and purpose are linked." We can't search for possibilities without finding greater purpose. To illustrate that, here are several examples:

- A customer service representative in a call center could say she answers phones. She will find her possibility by thinking about the purpose of her work. She delivers world-class service to hundreds of people every week. What possibilities will present themselves if she begins to think about her purpose rather than her task?

- The teller in a bank sees beyond a routine transaction, looking to the customer relationship. She realizes every customer interaction is an opportunity to anticipate and discover new ways to serve this customer financially. Her purpose is to meet financial needs, to create and sustain wealth. That unlocks new possibilities. It pushes her to a new level of performance.

- A supervisor believes her job is more than posting a schedule and monitoring her employees. She wants to build a team of committed people. When framed with purpose, her job explodes with possibility! She moves from policing people to developing them. That's an entirely different action plan.

Remember too that potential is a subjective thing. Does it surprise you to learn that men are more likely than woman to be selected for high-potential or accelerated development programs? "A recent report has found that the deck is stacked against working women from the earliest days of their careers, because female leaders are under-represented in accelerated development programs early in their careers, which hinders their climb up the ladder."[1]

This is a call to action! Women have amazing potential at work, but we must see the potential in ourselves before we can make it part of our brand and present its value.

PUBLIC SERVICE ANNOUNCEMENT

We must never imagine our potential is obvious. In order for it to be realized, it must first be recognized.

Where is your potential, and how is it hidden?

We've come full circle with that question. If you don't actively manage the zone of high performance, you will struggle to recognize and present potential. If you fail to do the work outlined here—branding, networking, negotiating, presenting value, and so on—your potential may not be apparent. Everything you have been reading about and working on has prepared you to demonstrate greater potential.

Questions like these may help you solve the potential mystery where you work.

1. Who is considered high potential?

2. What behaviors, skills, and attitudes are creating that perception?

3. Does your organization have a program for accelerated development?

4. If so, what are the criteria for consideration?

It is certainly possible to miss the potential inside of ourselves and within our circumstances. It's also possible to miss opportunity because sometimes "she" doesn't look like we've imagined her to be.

OPPORTUNITY IN DISGUISE

There is no question that opportunity will present herself. Will we recognize her when she arrives? I am learning that opportunity has a wardrobe filled with disguises. Sometimes opportunity just doesn't look like opportunity. If you aren't watching for her, she may brush right by you unnoticed.

I'm also learning that opportunity doesn't always knock. Sometimes, like wisdom, she waits in the wings and behind the scenes. For example:

- She attends the team meeting that has been derailed by excuses and negativity. Here you have the opportunity to be a positive catalyst that changes the course of the conversation with a game-changing question: What pieces of this problem do we control? Or, what options are available to us?

- Opportunity is available for that routine, mundane assignment. Here she might ask, "How can you add value to this? How can you make it better?"

- You'll find her as you greet the day, when you're grateful for the opportunity to begin again. Each day brings with it new "offers" and fresh opportunities.

- Notice her when you decide to break out of destructive patterns and make new choices for yourself.

- Find her in the moment you realize there are more options available to you. The possibilities really are endless.

- She may hide behind a persistent problem or inside the daunting task you've been putting off. She may dare you to try something new, or she might simply inspire you to begin.

- Opportunity will even dream with you big beautiful dreams about the future you can create.

Thinking about opportunity in this way changes where I look for her and what I think she looks like. I want to recognize her in all of her disguises. The question has never been whether or not opportunity will arrive, because she surely will. The challenge is spotting her in the crowd and maximizing the moment.[2]

Reports predict that women, once the minority in the workplace, are approaching and may surpass the number of men in the workforce.[3] Even though women are on the threshold of being the majority at work, they are still likely to earn less than men and occupy fewer executive positions.

I was discussing this with an executive I admire very much, and she put it this way: "The big question is whether or not women will maximize the opportunities presented in the workplace. Will they reach higher, showcase their talents, and use the resources available to them? Or will they fall into some of the old patterns such as trying to do it all themselves or thinking they must have every answer? Will they recognize opportunity when she brushes by them?"

MAKE AN INVESTMENT IN YOU

The work we have been doing together is an investment. You have spent time thinking about who you are and what you want to create. You've imagined a brand that is uniquely your own, and I hope your story is on the board!

As you reinvent or release a new version of you, clean out the emotional closet. Make this a new season in your life that is full of promise. Cast off the attitudes and beliefs that will steal your possibilities. This is not one of those "by-the-way-before-you-go" comments. Frankly, it is hard work to clean out the emotional closets. But if we don't, there will not be enough space for the things we want to add. Perhaps there is room for one more public service announcement.

PUBLIC SERVICE ANNOUNCEMENT

In order to grow, some things must go.

Part one of my book *Ready, Set . . . Grow!* is devoted to the arduous task of pulling out of our lives what will block, frustrate, and limit our growth. In those chapters you will learn how to capture and replace beliefs that are holding you back, break free of the worry habit, and manage toxic relationships effectively.

Pulling out of your life what doesn't work may sound like subtraction. I would also call it an investment. Here are some other ways I encourage you to make the investment in you:

1. Actively acknowledge your strengths by developing them. Like an artist or a musician, you are never finished perfecting your craft. Look for ways to grow "in your grain" in ways that are natural to you. Take your skills to the next level.

2. Buy the books and mark them up. I found my favorite copy of *Designed for Success* at a book signing in Houston. It is filled with markers and notes and highlights. I think this is exactly how it should look!

3. Take a class. Sign up for a workshop. Keep learning and looking for ways to apply what you have learned.

4. Reward yourself in meaningful ways. When you achieve a goal, celebrate!

5. Enlarge your comfort zone by trying something new.

6. Reflect more. What do you love about your life and work? What isn't working for you? What are you learning? How are you growing?

7. Pay attention, and allow yourself to be present in the moment. We can miss so much in the rush to check off the tasks and get it all done.

8. Make time for things that inspire and refresh you.

9. Find a way to give and allow yourself to receive and breathe more deeply.

Remember, paths are personal things, and the journey is just as important as the destination. Enjoy the trip! Allow yourself to fully experience the process of becoming. Once in a while, remember to rest and take in the view. Notice how far you've come and how much you've grown.

Whether you are jumping the tracks, reinventing your job, or pushing a boulder, I hope you will search for and develop your high-performance zone. You absolutely were designed for success and built to grow. As you implement the ideas presented here, I wish you all the best. I can't wait to see how your story unfolds, the difference you will make, and the value you will create. I'll be watching for your bold moves!

> May your path unfold before you like a gift;
> May you step out with confidence and do something amazing
>   with your life;
> May opportunity reveal herself to you;
> May wisdom dance on your stage,
> And may God bless your moves!

GET YOUR MOVE ON!

You are the talent. You are also the agent marketing and managing the opportunities. This week think like a talent agent, and find a way to invest in yourself.

Challenge yourself to recognize opportunity in all of her disguises. Where is "she" hiding within your circumstances?

Zoe has become a regular at the theater. She is known as an accomplished improviser. Experienced actors enjoy working with her because she is so skilled at sharing the focus and control of the scenes. New players appreciate her ability to guide and support them as they learn. She has mastered the art of receiving offers and advancing the scene.

She has also become a skilled mentor. As she reaches forward in her life, she is also reaching back to grasp the hand of others who are looking for a firm hold. On more than one occasion she has scribbled a quick note saying, "You are on the threshold! Call me if you want to maximize the opportunity that is waiting at your door." When the call comes, Zoe faithfully answers.

The agency has almost doubled in size. The new account, also known as "the mountain," has become the crown jewel, and the team has celebrated many milestone achievements. One by one the boulders have been moved and sculpted to create a monumental success.

Once in a while Zoe goes to the park and watches *parkour*, and she is a frequent guest at the coffee shop. The chairs no longer swallow her alive, but on more than one occasion she has seen them attempt to gulp others down.

She recognizes the look in their eyes as they try to balance precarious cups of coffee without spilling. She sees them glance around, imagining others are so much more assured and successful. Zoe remembers feeling like that, and she imagines almost everyone has felt that way at one time or another.

Alena has become more than a mentor. She is one of Zoe's dearest and most trusted friends. When they last met, Zoe had an announcement. "I know why you did it," she said matter-of-factly. "I wondered for the longest time, but now I know."

"Did what?" Alena laughed. "What have I done now?"

"When you first contacted me, I was astonished. I couldn't imagine why you would give me a second thought or make time to help me. It took being a mentor for me to understand why you invested so much of yourself in my success. You told me I would answer that question for myself, and now I can. It's wonderful to watch another person become."

Alena was quiet for a moment, and then she said, "I saw something in you, Zoe—something precious and powerful. You have such potential. It has been an honor to be a part of your process and to watch you become. Someone did that for me too. He reached right down and lifted my head just when I thought I had nothing of value to offer."

"I can't even imagine you being in that place, Alena," Zoe said, and she meant that. For her, Alena was a force of nature! She couldn't picture Alena as frightened, weak, or lost.

"Zoe, we've all been there. The question isn't whether we will someday need help. It's whether or not we will recognize it when it arrives. Will we be wise enough to receive it?"

Zoe knew this was true from her own experience and from observing Sara's last weeks at the agency. She had watched Sara furiously treading the water, unwilling to accept the lines thrown to her. "I didn't think I needed help in my first job," Zoe admitted. "I thought I was doing just fine right until I was fired!

"You didn't know what you didn't know, and you couldn't see what you weren't looking for," Alena answered. "If we are open and ask the right questions, the answers will come."

They were sitting in the coffee shop, and Zoe smiled, remembering their first meeting. It seemed like a lifetime ago. Thinking about the three questions, she smiled and said, "The answers do come."

"Have you heard the story 'Acres of Diamonds'?" Alena asked Zoe. "I have always loved it.

"A farmer hears an amazing tale of diamond mines that will make a man rich beyond every imagination. Even though he owns a large farm, he becomes discontent. Sadly, once he learned of the diamonds, he went to bed a poor man. He had lost nothing, but his life looked small and insignificant when held to the light of those jewels.

"Unable to think of anything else, the farmer sells his land and leaves his family behind to search for diamond mines. Ultimately he fails and destroys himself, but that isn't the end of the story.

"One day while watering his camel, the man who purchased the farm notices a brilliant flash of light in the shallow water of a brook. It was a huge diamond, and there were many, many more. 'For every acre of that old farm, yes, every shovelful, afterward revealed gems which since have decorated the crowns of monarchs.'4

"If only the farmer had looked for the diamonds in his own backyard! He would have realized the wealth he had only imagined.

"That happens in the workplace too. We can mistakenly believe things are so much better 'over there' without exploring the possibilities and opportunities right where we are. Anyone who has found a way to

195

move a boulder or reinvent her job will tell you there are gems waiting to be discovered in your current role."

"That's a wonderful story," Zoe replied. "Perhaps we prove ourselves ready for greater things when we have taken good care of what has been placed in our hands. It's ridiculous to reach for more when we haven't fully explored what is already ours."

Alena nodded as if to say, "Exactly right!"

Then she spoke, "Treasures are planted inside each of us. It's wonderful when we discover those and bring them into the light. That's what you've been doing in these last months. You've been unearthing the jewels that were both inside of you and inside of your circumstances."

They were quiet for a time, each of them thinking their separate thoughts and comfortable with the silence sitting between them. Zoe was thinking about this amazing journey called life. She was grateful for all of the experiences that led her to this place and this moment. She was thankful for Alena, who was such an unexpected blessing.

"You've done a beautiful job advancing the scene," Alena said, breaking the silence.

Just then, in the corner of her mind, Zoe glimpsed wisdom. She watched as wisdom took center stage and began to dance.

Appendix A

THE QUESTIONS I AM
MOST OFTEN ASKED

FOR SOME TIME now, I have been collecting my favorite workplace questions. These come from live appearances, my Web site, Twitter (@dondiscumaci), podcasts, e-mails, and media interviews.

I love these interactive pieces of my work. Questions like these keep me dialed in to what really matters. They keep it real. If you don't see yours here, I invite you to ask at www.dondiscumaci.com.

What can I do to market myself without sounding like I am bragging?

Women often tell me this is a challenge. As children we are taught not to brag. We hear things like don't brag, don't fight, and don't be bossy! All grown up now, we're trying to figure out how to market ourselves effectively. It is a paradox: we shrink from the idea of self-promotion, yet we are all expected to find acceptable ways of doing exactly that!

"Women often underplay what they've done, and the problem is when you do that, people will start to believe you. Women have to get better at promoting themselves—what they stand for, what

197

makes them different than someone else. They need to fight for their message," advises author Catherine Kaputa.[1]

This is so true! The first commandment in *Designed for Success* is, "Manage your message from the inside out." What we believe about ourselves becomes what we say to ourselves. That message turns outward as we present ourselves and ultimately is reflected in what others believe about us.

This inside-out process can work for or against you, and it begins with what you believe and say to yourself. That's why it is so important to carefully monitor your self-beliefs and self-talk. From there it's a matter of finding your story and learning how to tell it well.

Here are nine things you can do to craft your marketing message:

1. Find your niche and establish yourself as the "expert" by learning all you can, staying up to date, and sharing information others need and value. Market yourself by becoming a resource and by helping others become more successful. The key to this tip really is the sharing part. Having information doesn't make you a resource; sharing it does. Think river, not reservoir. A river flows and brings life. A reservoir holds and collects.

2. Shine the spotlight on others. Be generous in giving others credit and appreciation. It's amazing to watch the credit you have given away come back to you multiplied and pressed down.

3. If you make a mistake, talk about what you learned from the experience and the action you have taken to correct the course. People will remember the

action long after they forget the error. They will also remember your willingness to take responsibility.

4. Be ready to tell your success stories. Collect your success stories, and learn how and when to tell them. Once you have isolated your stories, you might be surprised at how often they are relevant to the conversation.

5. Link your stories with your brand. Let's say you want to be known as creative, resourceful, and strategic. What stories or examples reflect those characteristics? How have you demonstrated these attributes in your work? (Incidentally, you will want to be intentional about using brand words in your stories. Here's how that might sound, "This was a great strategic exercise. I loved working on this because it was such a challenge; it required me to be creative and resourceful.")

6. Instead of talking about a weakness, talk about what you are interested in learning and how you are growing. What a difference this makes. Instead of proclaiming, "I've never been good with details," lead with your strength by declaring, "I am a big-picture person; that has always been natural for me. I am learning how to value and manage the details too."

7. Don't throw your "promotions" away! When someone compliments you, receive it graciously. This is yet another example of the inhaling and exhaling, giving and receiving. When you throw back a compliment by underplaying your results, you block the flow.

8. Pay attention to your presentations, even the spontaneous hallway "drive-bys." How do you talk about yourself, and what you are working on?

9. Remember, introductions are like personal commercials. When you meet new people, is your thirty-second promo ready to go?

Before we can do any of these things, we must give ourselves permission to reflect value. As you can see, this isn't learning how to brag. (We must stop thinking about promotion in that way.) This is learning how to present yourself. It is forging your brand, building credibility, and finding ways to help others succeed. It is making your progress more visible and your results more obvious.

How do I find a mentor?

In Zoe's story, the mentor Alena found her. That happens sometimes. Mentors see something in us that resonates, and they step into the situation. Perhaps in those moments they are seeing a previous version of themselves, and they can deeply relate to where we are. Or they may recognize untapped potential and understand how to draw it out.

It's wonderful when that happens, but we can't wait for our mentors to appear. It's important to be proactive in searching for them.

1. Look for mentors with the skills and abilities you want to acquire. Who does what you want to do well? Who has mastered the skills you are trying to cultivate?

2. Present your greatest challenge as a mentoring case study. (I call this "drive-by" mentoring, because it happens in real time.) Honestly, the challenge you

are facing right now may be the doorway to your mentoring experience.

3. Go where your potential mentors are—associations, networking events, and workshops. Consider mastermind groups, book discussion clubs, and volunteer work. Look for and create opportunities to synchronize your networking and mentoring strategies.

4. Because mentoring relationships are based on trust, it is important to seek out mentors who share your values, people who are respected and admired. Look for people with strong, positive brands.

5. Perhaps the best advice is to make room for a different format of mentoring. Look inside and outside of the organization you work for. Does it surprise you to learn your colleagues and peers may not work for the company you do? Blow through the mind-sets that lead you to believe your peers are only the people you work with. Your mentor may not live in your town or even your country.

You may have many mentors in your life. Some of these will become lifelong friendships. Others won't. They will be for a season and a specific purpose. That is perfectly fine.

Once I find a mentor, how do I make the most of the mentoring experience?

This is a great question!

The best mentoring is based on the needs of the protégé or mentee. We choose mentors who will work in context with our goals and values. It is also protégé driven. That means we don't wait for wisdom to drip from the lips of our mentors! We must give them something to work with.

Think for a moment about the process of working a jigsaw puzzle. You study the picture on the lid of the box and set it in a prominent place (so you can refer to it often). Then you search for the straight edges to build the frame. Inside that framework you begin to fit the pieces together.

Mentoring is like a jigsaw in many ways. There is some structure to it. The framework is built by agreeing on what you are trying to accomplish, how you will measure success, and identifying action steps to achieve the goals.

The greatest difference (or challenge) between mentoring and the puzzle is this: there is no picture on the lid of the career box! There may be many ways to put the pieces together, and how you do that creates a unique portrait. You might find some of the pieces just don't fit into the bigger vision, and you may need to reshape or add pieces to complete the picture.

To make the most of a mentoring experience, protégés must bring their pieces and put them on the table. The pieces include many of the things we've been discussing here—strengths, talents, brand, experiences, goals, and challenges. This is the data mentors use to help you work the puzzle.

Do your homework, and put your pieces on the table to make the most of your mentoring experiences.

How can I handle a negative co-worker?

Negative people drain the life out of everything they touch! My first advice is to avoid them altogether. Remove yourself. If that isn't possible, you'll need to have your scripts ready.

In chapter 8 of my book *Ready, Set...Grow!* you'll find three important scripts for the toxic people in our lives. "We don't always get to choose whom we work with or for. We do control how we interact with the people in our personal and professional lives. We control our boundaries and our scripts."[2]

For the negative co-worker, stop the toxic flow by acknowledging her diplomatically. That sounds like, "I can see you are very frustrated." This is not agreement or sympathy! It is a verbal stop sign. Follow your acknowledgement by asking a solutions-oriented question. For example:

1. How do you want this to turn out?

2. What do you need to feel better about this situation?

3. What are you doing to meet that need?

4. What options do you have?

5. What have you tried (or what are you willing to try)?

Questions like these point to the future. They ask for accountability, and they don't enable victim-like behavior.

One of two things will happen when you have your scripts ready. You will help someone break out of a negative cycle, or she will stop dumping her toxic load in your lap (because solutions are no fun when you want to whine). Either outcome is perfectly OK with me!

How do you deal with office gossip?

Make yourself absolutely unavailable for this kind of communication! It's important that you do so because engaging in these conversations reinforces one of the worst female stereotypes and weakens your brand.

We all know people who are more or less town criers. They love to share the latest shocking tidbits. I laugh when gossip is cloaked in concern: "I am so worried about Sue because I heard..."

News bulletins also require a script. My all-time favorite response goes something like this: "I would be devastated if someone said that about me." If you use this one, prepare for an awkward silence, hold steady, and resist every temptation to ease the tension.

If that doesn't do the trick, you may need a more direct approach. Hold up your hand (like a stop sign) and tell the reporter, "I am sure if she wants me to know this, she will tell me herself." (If the thought of saying this horrifies you, don't worry; you won't need to say it often. People will quickly learn you do not appreciate this kind of "news," and they will stop bringing you the headlines.)

What if I am not getting the direction I need from my boss?

Many employees are not getting the direction or the feedback they need to feel prepared, valued, and successful. Not only is this frustrating, but it can also do a real number on your confidence and job satisfaction.

One employee described it to me this way: "I feel like an island. I am totally disconnected and cut off. I'm doing the best I can, but I'm not sure what the priorities are, and I don't know if I am succeeding. I hope no news really is good news."

Another variation on the theme is: "My boss is too busy to give me direction, feedback, or even train me to be more of a resource. His plate is spilling over. What a paradox: he's too busy to show me how I can help him. We just react all day long and put out the fires."

Scenarios like these take us right back to the high-performance zone. These are great examples of reaching for what you need rather than waiting for it to magically appear. When we are not getting enough direction, we have to develop perspective, demonstrate personal leadership, locate resources, and manage our capabilities accordingly.

Because bosses are busy, time with them may be a premium. You'll need to focus the conversation. Asking for "more direction" may not yield anything of real value, so plan to be specific.

Isolate the gray areas. Make a list of the situations where you feel like you are working in the dark. Then think about the end goals for these assignments:

- What does success look like in your mind?
- How will it be measured?
- What do you assume the expectations to be?
- What information are you missing?
- What resources will you need to accomplish the goal?

These are definitely perspective-challenging scenarios. When we are working "blindly," we don't understand the impact we are (or could be) having on the bigger picture. Before speaking with your manager, ask yourself perspective-building questions too.

- Who is affected by the work you do?
- Who must live with the decisions you make?
- How does your work touch the priorities of the organization?

Once you've answered questions like these to the best of your ability, share your thoughts with your boss. Ask her to validate your assumptions or help you correct the course.

Unfortunately, the challenge might be more than a busy boss. You may find your boss is lacking a sense of direction. It's hard to give someone something you don't have. If that turns out to be true, use the questions you've planned to "manage up" or coach your boss. You can actually cue your manager with questions to think differently about the work being done.

At first, you may not get exactly what you need. Patience may be required as your boss learns how to communicate more effectively.

This is another great case for mentoring! Mentors can help us sort it out and find our footing. If you are facing a situation like this, consider bringing it as a business case to your mentor or mastermind group.

How can I make the transition back to work after being "out of the game" for several years?

Welcome back! We've been waiting for you, and we can't wait to see what you create in this new season of your life.

One of the greatest barriers women face when trying to reenter the workforce is confidence. We may be tempted to discount our experience or even apologize for our absence. Women leave the workplace for many reasons. If you stepped off the career path to raise your family, for example, you have absolutely nothing to apologize for. You made a conscious, values-based decision. You have invested yourself deeply in the success of others, and you have learned some amazing things along the way. You have been working very hard on really important things!

As you plan for "reentry," remember to bring your experiences with you. You do have transferable skills. How you apply them may change, but your skills retain their worth. What, for example, have you been organizing, coordinating, planning, and troubleshooting? What projects have you been managing?

Without a doubt your experiences are valuable. Make them relevant by putting them into the context of your new goal. Renew your skills by presenting them in a new frame.

The wonderful thing about reentry is that you are not limited to what you've done in the past. This is a new season of your life! Explore the options. Search for them, and assume there are more. Challenge your assumptions about what is possible. You might even consider test-driving opportunities by doing some freelance or temporary work.

Don't be surprised (or discouraged) if you need to get your foot in the door. You might not rejoin the workforce at the same position or with the same title you left with. Things have certainly changed while you've been away. Give yourself permission to begin at a level that allows you to build momentum, forge a brand, and grow into your long-term goal.

Repeat after me, "I will not despise a small beginning! I will use small beginnings as starting blocks and launching pads."

The work we've been doing together here will help you get your strategy on. Here are five additional tips to get you started and boost your confidence:

1. Create a long-term goal for yourself, and develop an action plan with realistic steps to achieve it.

2. Research the fields you're interested in. Find out what is new and what is challenging for these industries. What skill sets are these employers looking for? What are the most successful people in the field doing differently?

3. Reconnect with former colleagues. This is a great way to jump-start your network and learn more about what has changed, what is valued, and where the best opportunities are.

4. Take classes to refresh your skills.

5. Volunteerism is another fabulous way to reconnect. Women who have stayed connected in their communities find it easier to transition back into the workforce. (That's a good message for women who are moving out of the workforce. Stay connected while you're away.)

PUBLIC SERVICE ANNOUNCEMENT

Stepping off the career stage doesn't mean you aren't
invited to the play.

Whatever the reason for your exit and your reentry, I wish you the best of success as you create new possibilities for yourself. This can be a humbling experience, with a steep learning curve, *and* it is filled with the most wonderful possibilities.

How can I maximize the talents I have?

I love this question, and I encourage each one of us to ask it of ourselves—frequently.

Your God-given strengths and talents are essential to your high-performance zone, and you will flourish when you operate in them. We all move more naturally and effectively when we use our gifts. But how often do we discount or take for granted what comes naturally for us? Things you do intuitively—what comes easily to you—are your assets.

Here are five things you can do to find, grow, and market your talents:

1. Locate and acknowledge your gifts. Pull them out of the dusty corners, polish those skills, and let them shine! Make a list of your strengths, and think about how you are using them to succeed.

2. Look for more ways to apply your strengths and talents to the priorities of the organization. Use them to solve a problem or leverage an opportunity.

3. Ask for opportunities to use your strengths. This is a marketing message, and it might sound something

like, "I enjoy organizing and planning. How could I use those skills to help this team (or company) accomplish more?"

4. Look outside your day-to-day responsibilities for special projects, or find a "boulder" to push (as described in chapter 6). Your talents might shine more brightly working on a special project.

5. Check your brand. Are your talents showing? Are they what you are known for? Do your talents make you top of mind for the assignments you would enjoy working on? Be intentional with building a brand that showcases your gifts.

Is there a place for my faith at work?

The short answer is ... absolutely. Here's the longer version.

Your faith is not something you put on and take off like a business suit. If you can remove it circumstantially, I wouldn't call it faith. *Duty* might be a better word. Your faith is who you are. I am very weary of the political correctness game. We go so far out of our way not to offend anyone, ever. God forbid someone might not agree with my position.

PUBLIC SERVICE ANNOUNCEMENT

If you don't stand for anything, eventually you will just fall over.

My work is deeply rooted in my faith, and I won't apologize for that. God is the source of my strength. My talents are the gifts He has given to me. My opportunities come from His hand. My work is the gift I give to Him.

I've learned the hard way that I cannot trust in my own strength and ability. I need God to accomplish the purposes planted by Him in my heart. I've seen the difference between what I can do on my own and what He can do through me. I can't always trust in my abilities, but I can always trust in His.

I work in the corporate sector. My faith equips and inspires me to be excellent. It makes me better. My clients may not know it, but I pray for them. I pray for their success and prosperity. I pray for wisdom and insight as I work with them. And God answers those prayers.

Faith at work is not a badge. It isn't lecturing, judging, or preaching. (That's not only annoying, but it's also inappropriate.) It is walking in the absolute confidence that the One who created everything is working for you and through you. You are designed for success and built to grow! Sometimes I think the best advice is to RELAX! Let your faith be the more natural part of who you are.

Two More Real-Life Takeaways to Get You Moving

In writing this book, I started a new collection of stories about women who have mastered the moves. From the front lines to executive suites around the world, I am asking women to share their experiences.

You've met some of them already. They inspire us to move boulders, negotiate for greater wins, manage our brands, and reinvent our jobs. They remind us to network, mentor, and mastermind. Below are two more examples, and the collection continues to grow. Visit www.dondiscumaci.com to read the stories or share your own.

Let what you value guide you

After the birth of her daughter, Liz was determined to design a life that allowed her to succeed personally and professionally. Success in her personal life meant not having someone else raise her daughter while she was working at a traditional job. She formulated a plan to build a business, which began in what she calls the "third bedroom."

Liz saw the exit sign clearly and stepped boldly through that door. Today she is the president of a successful training company. She is doing what she loves, and she's very good at it. When I asked Liz what she was thinking as she made the leap, her answer was spontaneous. "It's what I didn't think about that made the difference."

I love that! What we don't think about is just as important as what we do think about. Liz didn't spend weeks poring over the risk of her decision. She trusted her capabilities and found a way to align her experience with her values. "I got on the phone, sold some training, and off we went," she told me.

As I spoke with her, I realize how strategic she really was. Her company didn't launch on a whim. It was born from her willingness to step out and make something marvelous happen.

Use adversity as a catalyst

Trina's move wasn't voluntary. She was shoved out the door in a massive layoff with only hours of notice. "It was horrible and humbling," she told me. "At first, my goal was to replace the job I'd lost by looking for similar work. Then I realized this was an opportunity to do something completely new. It was a chance for me to do something I'd always been interested in—law."

Trina took a temporary assignment at a law firm. With her foot firmly in the door, she studied for her paralegal certification and concentrated on building a network within the legal field. She

211

proved herself quickly and, within a year, moved from a temporary to a full-time position.

Her long-term plan is a law degree and a private practice. Every day Trina moves a little closer to her vision. "I not only have a storyboard," she laughs, "but I've also already designed my future office. The work I am doing now is equipping me for my long-term vision, and I have great mentors to help with my homework."

Trina offers this advice: "No matter what happens outside of you, find your center inside of a big dream."

Appendix B

FOR BOSSES ONLY

What Your Employees Desperately Want You to Know

THIS IS SOMETHING I hear at almost every conference: "I wish my boss were here. He really needs to hear this!" Right behind that comment is this one: "It's hard to implement strategies like these when your boss doesn't understand or support them." In other words, I won't be putting any of this into practice because my boss doesn't get it. Until she gets it, I can't be effective.

Pure bunk!

These comments rev my engine, because we must get to a place where we stop worrying about who isn't in the room! When we are listening for the messages others need to hear, we are missing our own.

I do understand the frustration. When I speak about anger management, the angry people usually aren't there. The people in the room are the ones trying to cope with angry people. It's a paradox—the people who need it the most may not ever come.

Even so, there is only one person you can change, and that person is you. It's never our job to change another person. It's our responsibility to manage ourselves. Sometimes when we change our approach, we will get a new response. It's wonderful when that happens, but we don't get credit for changing the other person. We've just unlocked the doors, broken the cycle, and invited a more effective response.

In the spirit of public service announcements, I've put together a bosses-only collection. These are the things employees tell me they wish they could say to their bosses. It's certainly not a one-size-fits-all collection, but if you are a boss and find this page bookmarked or highlighted in the employee lounge, it may be your sign!

Dear Boss:

1. I am motivated. Honestly I am. I have bills to pay, kids to feed, and dreams to dream. I am motivated by the values I carry with me and by the things I want to do, have, and become. Please do not think your job is to motivate me. I'd rather have you focus on recognizing what knocks the wind out of my sails! What gets in my way and prevents me from making real progress. What discourages me. What are the de-motivating forces at work here.

2. When you walk by me in the hallway without saying a word, what does that mean exactly? Are you deep in thought, disappointed in my work, or just too busy? Incidentally, nods and smiles are free, take just a second, and would save me a whole lot of guess-work. When I am trying to figure you out, I am not

focusing on the things that make this organization go.

3. Involve me! I have good ideas, and I want to share them.

4. I want to learn how to solve problems and make better decisions. When you give me the answers—as right as those answers may be—I am borrowing your judgment rather than creating my own. Help me grow by encouraging me to think for myself.

5. When you take credit for my work, I absolutely want to scream!

6. Tell me what you need, but please, please let me figure out *how* to make it happen. When you micro-manage tasks, I stop thinking for myself because I am trying so hard to think like you.

7. Connect me with the bigger picture. Help me understand the difference I am making with my projects and assignments. I want to feel valuable and valued.

8. When you count my minutes, you encourage me to count yours. I wish we worried less about clocks and more about results.

9. When it comes to change, even when you can't tell me everything, please tell me what you know. Tell me what you can. Trust me with your truth.

10. It's been a really long time since I felt truly appreciated.

11. Sometimes I think you're afraid of me or afraid that I will outgrow, outshine, or outperform you. I don't

understand that at all. Isn't the essence of leadership to create success? The more successful I am, the
more successful you are. My success is your success,
right?

12. E-mail isn't always the best way to communicate
with me. I wish we had more honored and uninter-
rupted time to talk.

13. When you make an appointment with me, I structure my day around it. Let's just say, it's a priority in
my calendar. I understand you are busy and things
come up, but I wish your appointments with me
were less of an option for you.

14. If you were more comfortable giving feedback, I
think I would be more comfortable receiving it.
Sometimes my performance review feels more like a
form to be completed than a conversation about my
contributions and a plan to develop. I have feedback
too. Please ask me for it.

15. I am wired to win, and given the opportunity, I will.

Here are some points that will make the boss smile! These
comments, also from employees, would go best on a thank-you
card.

1. Thank you for trusting me with important tasks and
assignments. I don't take that lightly. Sometimes I
think you believe in me more than I believe in me.
That is incredibly motivating. I would never want to
let you down.

2. I appreciate it when you challenge my thinking
with questions instead of answers. (I fully realize

you are asking me questions you wish I were asking of myself!) In the process of searching for my own answers, I am developing judgment and confidence. It would be easier and faster for you to give me the "right" answer. Thank you for every time you've resisted that temptation.

3. You stand up for me, and I appreciate that.

4. I am proud to be on this team because you are so respected within the organization and you champion our projects so beautifully.

5. Thank you for modeling life-work balance. I value that too. Even though we work very hard around here, I know that you expect me to put my family first.

6. Thank you for making it safe for me to learn. Even when I make a mistake, I know you are more concerned with the learning part than the mistake part.

7. I love it that you hate excuses! You are not interested in explanations. Thank you for placing a premium on action and making it absolutely unnecessary to explain, justify, and defend.

8. You know every name in this department, and you make everyone here feel like an important part of the team. You may never know how much that means to me.

9. I appreciate it when you ask for my advice. It is motivating to be included in the plan.

10. It is very apparent that you have my best interests at heart. I appreciate what you are doing to prepare me for my next step. Thank you for challenging me to be more innovative with my plans and more focused with my career strategies.

11. Today you acknowledged my work. I really needed that. How did you know?

12. Thank you for creating such a positive working environment. Very much like weather, the climate you have established invites results. I appreciate that you have a very low tolerance for unproductive communication. Thank you for setting those expectations and modeling them every day.

CHAPTER DISCUSSION GUIDE

I'M A BIG believer in book clubs, so I'm thrilled to hear of *Designed for Success* and *Ready, Set...Grow!* discussion groups popping up around the world! In Birmingham, Boston, Seattle, Wichita, Dallas, Houston, and Nairobi are just of few of the groups I've personally interacted with. What a pleasure it has been to meet you in person and discuss these success principles with you.

If *Career Moves* makes the list for your book club or inspires you to start one, the following questions may help you get or keep the discussion going.

CHAPTER 1: MOVING SIGNS

1. Intentionally, physical descriptions of the characters are not provided. How do you picture Zoe and Alena? Why?

2. Which of the characters resonates with you most? What creates that connection for you?

3. Which of the moving signs can you relate to? What would you add to the list?

4. What do you think about the "new rules" for employees? Are you surprised by any of them? Would you add a rule?

5. How has your job changed in the past twelve months?

6. How have you changed?

7. How are you personally impacting the strategy of your organization?

8. What questions do you wish you had asked yourself five years ago?

9. Which of the four elements (perspective, leadership, capabilities, and resources) do you manage most naturally? Which is most challenging for you?

10. Why is Alena taking such an interest in Zoe's career?

CHAPTER 2: STRATEGIC MOVES

1. How would you answer the three questions?

2. What do you think of the comment, "By the time a job is publicly posted, it has already been filled"?

3. Which of the career-mapping tools intrigue you the most?

4. What other steps or tools would you recommend for plotting one's opportunity?

5. What plans do you have to update your résumé and get your name "above the fold"?

6. Which social networking tools have you explored or experienced?

7. Do you have a self-discovery story?

8. What do you think of the violinist "playing out of context" story?

9. Can you think of an example when you were working out of context?

10. How has mentoring impacted you personally or professionally?

CHAPTER 3: INSIDE MOVES

1. What do you think of the three reinvention stories?

2. How can you apply those themes to reinvent the job you have?

3. When does it make sense to move backward or sideways in your career? Do you have an example?

4. What advice do you have for someone who is trying to "jump the tracks"?

5. Why do you think a small advertising agency was selected for Zoe's temporary assignment?

6. What is the difference between your experience and your experiences? Which do you talk about the most?

7. What does it mean for you to be a free agent marketing a package of skills and experiences?

8. Self-disclosure is a powerful communication tool. Why is it so important to be intentional with disclosure?

9. What do you think of the team meeting and Alison's approach?

10. What are you noticing about Zoe now? How is she progressing, and what is she missing?

CHAPTER 4: BAD MOVES

1. Which of the career "corners" do you relate to the most?

2. How comfortable are you with conflict?

3. What would your "conflict management" script sound like?

4. With what emotional triggers do you identify? What is at stake for you in these situations? What do you need?

5. What are you doing to manage the politics and the grapevine at work?

6. Do you have an example of failing to move?

7. Have you ever been "stuck on the wheel"?

8. What do you think would happen if documentation wasn't an option?

9. Are you finding ways to exhibit the four factors and find your high-performance zone?

10. Do you think Zoe is painting herself into a corner?

CHAPTER 5: BOLD MOVES

1. What do you think of Zoe's proposal?

2. How might you incorporate the steps of the one-hundred-day plan?

3. How can you become more intentional in building your professional network?

4. Who is on your "C" list of people you want to meet?

5. What risks should you be taking?

6. Have you participated in a form of masterminding? How can you use the concepts of masterminding more intentionally?

7. What bold moves have you seen?

8. What will your next bold move look like?

9. What are the obstacles and barriers in your environment?

10. How can you apply the disciplines of *parkour* to be more successful?

CHAPTER 6: SELF-DEFINING MOVES

1. How is your work like improv theater?

2. What do your offers look and sound like?

3. How are you accepting or blocking your offers?

4. Have you become more consciously aware of your offers?

5. How can you apply the rules of improvisation to your scenarios?

6. What would you add to the discussion of how life and work are like improvisation?

7. What are you noticing about yourself in terms of giving and receiving?

8. What difference have the words "yes, and..." made in your personal and professional relationships?

9. Are you more aware of your "no, buts..."? What examples can you share?

10. How can you apply the boulder philosophy in your current role?

CHAPTER 7: MAKE YOUR MOVES COUNT

1. What advice would you give Zoe regarding the feedback she has received from Todd?

2. What is Zoe's current brand as compared to the one she is trying to build?

3. What labels are you wearing? How would you like them to change?

4. What do you find most challenging about building a brand?

5. What words will you put on your teleprompter or cue cards?

6. In what ways do you need to present your value more effectively?

7. How do you create wins for others without creating one for yourself?

8. How well did Zoe handle the situation with Todd and the team? Would you have done anything differently?

9. We have the advantage of "listening" to Zoe's self-talk. How active is your inner critic?

10. What is the most important thing Zoe has learned so far?

CHAPTER 8: EXIT SIGNS

1. When do you know it is time to go?

2. In what ways do we take our problems with us when we leave a job?

3. What do you think happened to Sara?

4. How would you score the conditions and agents of your job?

5. Which of these dimensions are most important to you, and how can you influence them?

6. What is your best tip for making a graceful exit?

7. Madeline's job has completely defined her. Can you relate to feeling that way? How can you avoid becoming what you do and nothing more?

8. How well do you think Zoe navigated the scene with Madeline? Why?

9. What are you noticing about Zoe now? How has she changed?

10. What are you discovering about yourself?

CHAPTER 9: INSPIRING MOVES

1. How do women in the workplace miss or mismanage opportunities?

2. Why do you think men are more likely to be involved in accelerated development or high-potential programs?

3. How does one demonstrate greater potential?

4. How has opportunity come to you in disguise?

5. What can we learn from talent agents?

6. How are you investing in yourself?

7. Wisdom had been standing backstage; what brought "her" forward?

8. How can women stay connected and involved even if they leave the workforce for a time? (How important do you think that really is?)

9. Which characters or stories resonate with you the most in this book? Why?

10. If Alena were to ask you a question, what do you imagine it would be?

APPENDICES

1. In what ways are you missing or managing opportunities to promote yourself?

2. What would you do differently if you really believed that what others believe about you is a reflection of how you have presented yourself?

3. Who are your mentors, and how did you find them?

4. What has mentoring meant for you?

5. What are your natural, God-given talents, and how are you using them intentionally?

6. What is your best tip for handling negativity and office gossip?

7. Where do you find your feedback, and how do you manage it?

8. What advice do you have for women who are moving back into the workforce?

9. How is your faith reflected in your work?

10. How would your letter to the boss read?

NOTES

Chapter 1—Moving Signs

1. Dondi Scumaci, *Designed for Success* (Lake Mary, FL: Excel Books, 2008), 1.
2. Jan Reid, "You and Your Who?" *AmericanWay*, September 1, 2009, http://www.americanwaymag.com/bob-beaudine-george-w-bush-texas-plano-recruiter (accessed November 25, 2009).
3. Susan Shinn and Lois Weber, "Kerry: Learning to Improve Engagement," *Talent Management*, March 2009, http://www.learnshare.com/v2/files/kerry.pdf (accessed November 25, 2009).
4. Bill Trahant, "Debunking Five Myths Concerning Employee Engagement: A Recent Report Debunks the Myths and Reveals Practices for Enhancing Individual Employee Effectiveness to Improve Organizational Performance," *The Public Manager* 36: (2007), http://www.questia.com/PM.qst?a=o&d=5020267052 (accessed November 6, 2009).
5. Dondi Scumaci, *Ready, Set... Grow!* (Lake Mary, FL: Excel Books, 2009), 178.
6. Ibid., 175.

Chapter 2—Strategic Moves

1. Rod Napier, Clint Sidle, and Patrick Sanaghan, *High Impact Tools and Activities for Strategic Planning* (New York: McGraw-Hill, 1997), 185–189.
2. "Mind Maps," BuzanWorld.com, http://www.buzanworld.com/Mind_Maps.htm (accessed October 27, 2009).
3. "About StrengthsFinder 2.0," http://strengths.gallup.com/110440/About-StrengthsFinder-20.aspx (accessed November 6, 2009).
4. "Johari Window," http://www.noogenesis.com/game_theory/johari/johari_window.html (accessed November 6, 2009).
5. SparkTalk, "Four Social Media Tools Equal Professional Hygiene Made Easy," CareerRealism.com, May 3, 2009, http://www.careerrealism.com/careerealism-tv-what-does-your-brand-say-about-you/ (accessed November 6, 2009).
6. Michael Porter, *What Is Strategy?* (n.p.: Harvard Business School Publishing Corporation, 1996).
7. Gene Weingarten, "Pearls Before Breakfast," *Washington Post*, April 8, 2007, W10, http://www.washingtonpost.com/wp-dyn/content/article/2007/04/04/AR2007040401721.html (accessed November 10, 2009).

Chapter 4—Bad Moves

1. Patrick Lencioni, *The Five Dysfunctions of a Team* (San Francisco: Jossey-Bass, 2002).
2. Papercut Project Monitoring, "Why I'd Rather You Go Play in the Traffic," December 7, 2009, http://vimeo.com/8045199 (accessed January 4, 2010).
3. Michael Lombardo and Robert W. Eichinger, *FYI: For Your Improvement* (n.p.: Lominger Limited, Inc., 1996–2004).
4. Robin Fischer Roffer, *Make a Name for Yourself* (New York: Broadway Books, 2002), 107.
5. Scumaci, *Designed for Success*, 201–211.

Chapter 5—Bold Moves

1. Reid, "You And Your Who?"
2. Ibid.
3. John Funnell, "Facebook, Twitter, LinkedIn, Ulitzer, MeettheBoss—Execs Go Online Big-Time," Web 2.0 Journal, November 12, 2009, http://web2.sys-con.com/node/981804 (accessed November 12, 2009).
4. Adapted from Bert Decker, *You've Got to Be Believed to Be Heard* (n.p.: St. Martins, 1991). This is also available as an audiobook: Bert Decker, *How to Build Charisma, Credibility, and Trust* (n.p.: Nightingale Conant Audio, n.d.).
5. Napoleon Hill, "The Law of Success," 16 lessons, 1928, printed in book form as Napoleon Hill, *The Law of Success in 16 Lessons* (n.p.: The Design House, 2007).
6. Napoleon Hill, *Think and Grow Rich* (n.p., 1937); reprinted by Marketplace Books, 2007. Updated versions of this title are available.
7. Frank Farnschlaeder, "Research Report: On the Role of Coaching and Coaches in Mastermind Groups," MastermindGroups.info, October 2007, http://www.mastermindgroups.info/research-report/ (accessed November 6, 2009).
8. Case study from CB&I, Houston, Texas, August 2009.
9. Living Your Vision is the signature inviteCHANGE course. For more information, visit their Web site at http://www.invitechange.com/personal-development/living-your-vision.html.
10. Scumaci, *Ready, Set...Grow!* 122–124.
11. Patricia Walston, "Sarah Palin: She's Not 'Retreating; She's Reloading,'" *Atlanta Woman to Woman Examiner*, November 19, 2009, http://www.examiner.com/x-26504-Atlanta-Woman-to-Woman-Examiner~y2009m11d19-Sarah-Palin-She-is-not-retreating-shes-reloading (accessed November 24, 2009).

Chapter 6—Self-Defining Moves

1. Mark Bergen, Molly Cox, and Jim Detmar, *Improvise This!* (New York: Hyperion, 2002), 7.

2. ImprovComedy.org, "A Glossary for Improv Terms," http://www.improv comedy.org/glossary.html (accessed November 6, 2009).

3. Bob Burg and John David Mann, *The Go-Giver* (New York: Portfolio, 2007), 129.

4. Ibid., 107.

5. Stephen R. Covey, *First Things First* (n.p.: Free Press, 1996).

6. Author interview with Chip Ray, Executive Vice President, CB&I, Houston, TX, on August 12, 2009.

7. Ibid.

8. C. S. Lewis, *Selected Literary Essays* (n.p.: Cambridge, 1969).

Chapter 7—Make Your Moves Count

1. Roffer, *Make a Name for Yourself*, 2.

Chapter 8—Exit Signs

1. As referenced in Robert C. Beck, *Motivation: Theories and Principles* (n.p.: Prentice Hall, 2003).

2. Seth Godin, *The Dip* (New York: Portfolio, 2007), 4.

Chapter 9—Inspiring Moves

1. LawyersWeekly.com, "High Potential Programs Hinder Women," May 5, 2009, http://www.lawyersweekly.com.au/blogs/hr_news/ archive/2009/05/05/high-potential-programs-hinder-women.aspx (accessed November 5, 2009).

2. Adapted from Dondi Scumaci, "Opportunity Undercover," http://www .dondiscumaci.com/blog/2009/07/opportunity-undercover/ (accessed November 12, 2009).

3. Dennis Cauchon, "Women Gain as Men Lose Jobs," *USA Today*, September 3, 2009, http://www.usatoday.com/news/nation/2009-09-02-womenwork_ N.htm/ (accessed November 5, 2009).

4. Russel Herman Conwell, *Acres of Diamonds* (New York: Harper and Brothers, 1915), http://www.americanrhetoric.com/speeches/rconwellacres ofdiamonds.htm (accessed November 6, 2009).

Appendix A—The Questions I Am Most Often Asked

1. Anita Bruzzese, "On the Job: Women in the Workplace," USAToday.com, June 18, 2009, http://www.usatoday.com/money/workplace/2009-06-18 -on-the-job_N.htm (accessed November 6, 2009). Catherine Kaputa is the author of *The Female Brand* (n.p.: Davies-Black Publishing, 2009).

2. Scumaci, *Ready, Set...Grow!* 64.

You Were Designed for Success and Built to Grow! Get a Move On!

dondi
SCUMACI.inc

You are personally invited to visit www.dondiscumaci.com to get connected, stay energized, and do what you were built for... succeed! Stop by soon to explore these free tools and resources:

- **High-Impact Tips**
- **Blogs and Insights**
- **Podcasts for Inspiration on the Go**
- **Interviews with Women Who Are Making Bold Moves**
- **Event News**
- **Storyboard Showcase**
- **Zoe's Journal**

Bring Dondi to your organization this year!

If you would like to bring Dondi to your organization, please visit www.dondiscumaci.com for details on booking information and availability.

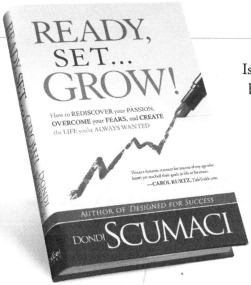
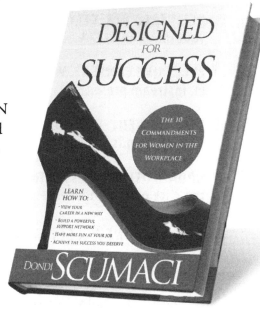